WHAT'S HAPPENING TO MY TEEN?

MARK GREGSTON

Foreword by JIM BURNS

HARVEST HOUSE PUBLISHERS

EUGENE, OREGON

WHAT'S HAPPENING TO MY TEEN?
Copyright © 2009 by Mark Gregston
Published by Harvest House Publishers
Eugene, Oregon 97402
www.harvesthousepublishers.com

Library of Congress Cataloging-in-Publication Data
  Gregston, Mark
  What's happening to my teen? / Mark Gregston.
    p. cm.
  ISBN 978-0-7369-2444-3 (pbk.)
    1. Parenting—Religious aspects—Christianity. 2. Parent and teenager—Religious aspects—Christianity. 3. Christian teenagers—Religious life. I. Title.
  BV4529.G734 2009
  248.8'45—dc22

                             2008049426

■ ■ ■ ■

To all the families who have entrusted
me through the years with their teens.

You have taught me much.

■ ■ ■ ■

Acknowledgments

This book is but a reflection of lessons I've learned and stories I've experienced working with teens throughout the years. They have taught me what works and what doesn't work. They have showed me what is effective and what is not. And they have touched my life in ways I never would have imagined. So first, I want to thank every young person who has trusted this mustached man with a big nose. You have schooled me well.

I would also like to acknowledge and thank a very special group of young people who met with me for a long time and shared their insights, thoughts, comments, and lives so I could glean wisdom for others. Special thanks to Katie Sanford, Jesse Guidry, Bri Bale, Megan Dunklin, Lily Cloninger, Max Doster, Shelby McGee, Blair Lackey, Katie Slater, Casey Hammons, Brittney Sglav, Taylor Schulz, Sarah McCleister, Emily Anderson, and Shely Kocijan.

A special thank you to Sam Satterwhite and Larry Bennett of Satterwhite Log Homes, two people who have made the Heartlight residential facility a warm and inviting place by building all of the log structures on the Heartlight property. You have helped us create an environment that offers help and hope to weary wanderers looking for a place of rest. In these buildings, lives have changed, hearts have been touched, and the lessons revealed within these pages have been learned.

To all the staff I have the honor to work with, I say thank you for your servants' hearts and your passionate fervor to be involved in the lives of the teens who live with us. Blake and Melissa Nelson, your caring heart for teens and their families is an extension of God's hand into their lives. Ben Weinert and Emily Roberts, your commitment to be involved in the lives of teens when it's not the most fun is admirable (and such a blessing to me!). To our counseling staff, Tony Michael, Ashley Michael, and Susan Lewis, your hearts truly are as big as Texas. Thanks to all of you for your offering to families and teens.

To Dave Bolthouse, Tammee Bolthouse, and Sam Sheeley, thank you for all the work you do to help get the message of hope out to parents and teens who need to hear it.

Thank you to all the Harvest House folks who are a part of making this book happen. And thanks also to Natalie Gillespie, who helps straighten out my thoughts when I get my mords wixed up and helps me put my thoughts in an order that others can understand.

Thank you, thank you, thank you to the Heartlight Ministries board of directors and the Heartlight Ministries foundation board for helping to make it all happen.

And last, but by no means least, thanks to my wife, Jan, whose heart of gold is seen by everyone and whose ability to lose anything and everything is a source of joy and laughter for us all.

Contents

Foreword

■ ■ ■ ■

can't think of a more qualified person to write this book than Mark Gregston. He knows teenagers as few people do, and he has been inside their heads and hearts for most of his adult life. Too many parents are not as ready for their kids' teen years as they think. (That was the case for Cathy and me.) For many teenagers, the transition from dependence on parents to independence is not easy, and most parents hit some rough spots along the way as well.

I have spent my entire adult life in youth and family ministry. I never dreamed the teen years with our own kids would be as stress-filled and humbling as they were. I still remember the day Christy, my oldest, didn't want to get out of the car and go get a treat with me because "There are boys in there, and I don't want them to see me with you." *Ouch!* Raising teenagers is humbling and challenging to say the least.

I want to congratulate you for picking up this book, because you can't afford to slow down with your parenting as your kids become teens. The stakes are just too high, and the risks are too prevalent in our culture. Sure, we were 13, 15, and 17 once, but we were never our kids' age because of this ever-changing culture. As parents, now is the time to hone our skills and reevaluate how we are doing with our teenagers. Mark, and this book, can help mentor you along the way. The teen years can stretch your faith and challenge your own marriage, but don't worry—most kids grow up and become responsible adults who will rise up and thank you someday.

Here are four quick thoughts as you begin.

You are not their friend. You are their parent. Act like a parent. You can't be their friend. They think you are too old anyway! Kids today need parents who will realize that their job is not to be their buddies but to give them loving and firm expectations so they will become responsible adults.

Nobody said it would be easy. If you are having an easy time of parenting, something could be wrong. The majority of parents of teenagers say that it is one of the most difficult tasks they have ever encountered. Don't let these years tear at the fiber of your marriage (if you are married), and don't be afraid to seek help. The Bible's advice about war applies to teens as well: "For lack of guidance a nation falls, but many advisors make victory sure" (Proverbs 11:14).

Most teenagers will test the limits. Many young people go through an experimental phase. Unfortunately, most kids will have to temporarily lose some of the values they have been taught in order to find their own. One of my daughters in college said, "I had to reject my parents' faith to own my own faith." Remember that the fruit usually doesn't fall far from the tree. If your kids rebel, set boundaries and discipline with consistency, but don't freak out. We all learn from our mistakes and failures.

God cares. Jesus wept at the death of a friend, and He cares deeply for hurting kids and parents. God promised that He will never leave you or forsake you. I appreciate Mark's reminder that God is present in the redemption of human beings, even challenging teenagers.

One day you will be able to use your experiences to help someone else understand why teens act the way they do. This is Mark Gregston's turn to give you some guidance. This book is filled with wisdom and insight from cover to cover.

Jim Burns
President, HomeWord

Introduction

■ ■ ■ ■

Did you wake up this morning and notice that your little girl is no longer the innocent little princess you used to throw around in the backyard pool? Has your son's demeanor changed and left you longing to see the little boy you used to know?

Have you just found out some bad news about your child's behavior, leaving you with your jaw dropped, wondering what happened? Have you ever wondered how the early years of raising your kids went so right, but the teen years seems to be going so wrong? Have you sat back with your cup of coffee in the morning and thought about today's teen culture and silently whispered to yourself how glad you are that you don't have to grow up in this generation? Have you begun to feel like a failure because the direction your child is headed looks different from what you had hoped for? Did you trust a parenting system that you now know you should not have trusted? Have you noticed changes in your teen and spent time praying that he'll just hold on to what he knows to be true? Have you lain awake at night, thinking to yourself, *What's happening to my teen?*

Your teen's world is far different from the world you grew up in. Today's teen culture is full of confusing values and misguided principles. It is saturated with the sexualization of our daughters and the mastication of our sons. The media is wrought with gossip-laden conversations, and it encourages competition in presentation, possessions, and experimentation. Life has sped up so much that we see communication without connection, relationship without commitment, and a demand for instant gratification with no effort. Society's moral standards have deteriorated. Entitlement and selfishness surround our teens, and the desire for more is never ending. New lifestyles are permissible and prevalent.

Teens' world is tough, and they need guidance, wisdom, and personal dedication from parents who already have full and busy lives. Parents' well-meaning intention to provide their children with a better life by giving them everything has helped create a generation of non-workers who want more and work less. Immaturity and irresponsibility abound. Yes, out teens' world is far different from the world most of us grew up in.

Less maturity, coupled with greater exposure to the world's offerings and demands, has influenced kids' choices, beliefs, values, and perceptions of others. Kids mature slower now, but they are exposed to more, so they sometimes don't have the resources to respond wisely when choices are forced on them. As a result, they suffer the consequences.

Parental involvement is critical in teens' lives. But in too many instances, parents have mistaken this need for an opportunity to hover over their lives and become overly involved and overprotective. This mind-set of parents enables teens to remain in the immaturity they seek to grow out of as parents provide their teens with more but don't prepare them for adult life. Teens want their parents involved in their lives to help them prepare for the world in which they will live. They want to develop a healthy independence.

When parents see the investment in their child's life stop giving any returns, when they feel as if their kids have rejected the seeds of Christian values sown in their lives, too many withdraw, feeling they have failed or been misguided. And teens, now left unprepared and alone, are overcome by the culture's influence on their lives at alarming rates. Teens are lost, and parents don't know what to do.

Most teens' fallen behavior is wrongly interpreted as rebellion. Throughout my 34 years of working with struggling teens, I've seen just about every type of behavior that parents don't want to child display. I used to label all unacceptable behaviors as reb\ and I could tout enough Scripture to justify my responses to it. N ertheless, through the years, I've come to understand that what I see is not necessarily what is. What most people see as rebellion is really something quite different. I wish I had known this in my earlier years of working with teens because it would have changed my approach, my attitude, and the outcome of my interactions. Reflecting on the hundreds of young people who have lived with us in our residential counseling program, I would now say that most of the ones display-ing inappropriate behavior were not rebelling at all. They were merely responding to situations they weren't prepared for.

So, the question that every parent must ask is this: Is the inap-propriate and unacceptable behavior I see in my teen rebellion, or is it a response to something that is happening or has happened in my child's life? Once you know the answer, you can understand how to pursue your child and engage in a way that stops the behavior and encourages growth within your family.

Rebellion has many different faces. The face we see on our teen may look like that of a rebel, but I have found that most of the time it is just an outward reflection of something on the inside that is good and understandable but that is displayed in an inappropriate way. If parents turn away from their teens because of the dastardly appear-ance of their teens' behavior, they might miss the true hearts of their children and the opportunity to speak truth to them during a time of struggle and difficulty. Sadly, the behavior will then continue.

Many parents spend so much time *correcting* their child that they forget the greater need their child is longing for—*connection*. The connection between parent and child is what reveals the true heart behind appropriate and inappropriate behaviors. If parents would spend more time trying to understand their children rather than trying to change them, the behavioral changes they hope for would be more likely to happen.

The purpose of this book is to assist you to go beyond what you see and to look into the heart of your teen. I will share other families' real-life stories and struggles so you can learn how to move toward your child's heart at the time when your teen needs your love and involvement the most. You can help your teen through this difficult and painful time rather than allow your teen to remain in it.

Through these stories, I hope to help you understand your child better so you can accurately and effectively handle what is in front of you. I hope to help you look beyond your child's behavior to see what is really happening in his life. I hope to bring clarity to the confusion that may be present in your home. I want to assist you to create an atmosphere of relationship that welcomes change, encourages maturity, and acknowledges growth.

These chapters contain stories of families' true experiences with a particular attitude or behavior that might be construed as rebellion, shares insights into that behavior or attitude, and gives some practical advice and scriptural insight for dealing with the issue at hand. Understanding is an essential element of knowing what to do when you encounter behavior that sometimes appears to be rebellion. Finally, we'll look at strategies that will empower your teen to change.

Chapter 1

When It Is and When It Isn't

■ ■ ■ ■

Believe it or not, you can't judge a teen by his behavior any more than you can judge a book by its cover. What you see is not what you always get, and just because something looks one way doesn't mean it is that way. Such is the world of teenage rebellion.

My wife, Jan, and I had just settled into our seats on a morning flight when I noticed a big, burly fellow sitting in the row in front of us, baseball cap pulled down on his head and bifocal glasses on his nose. The man was huge. I don't mean fat—I mean big. Just looking at this sixtyish, really large—but not athletic-looking—guy made me feel small. Through the seats, Jan noticed another man seated next to him. He was a younger, athletic-looking, muscular guy who was dressed sharply and didn't mind showing off his massive, well-defined arms. I peeked at him and thought, *The younger guy is a baseball player, and the other guy is his agent.* But remember, you can't judge a book by its cover.

Halfway through the flight, the muscular man pulled out an alternative-lifestyle magazine. Jan's eyes got big, and the big guy sitting next to the man with the magazine was clearly agitated as graphic pages flashed for all to see. The older guy stood up, dug around in his bag in the overhead bin and pulled out a book titled *Archeological Evidence for the Old Testament.* As he sat down, I recognized him under the ball cap. He was a retired NFL quarterback—one of the all-time best. (I'll call him Q.B.)

I chuckled as I realized then that they weren't together. Q.B. was one of the greatest athletes of all time, and the two had to sit next to each other for the remainder of the flight. One read his alternative-lifestyle magazine, and the other read his book on the Bible. And to think that I thought they were together. I chuckle even as I write that now.

Q.B. couldn't keep focused on the book he was reading, so I tapped him on the shoulder and asked if he wanted to read one of mine. (Okay, I admit, I was hoping to get a copy of my book *When Your Teen Is Struggling* in his hands.) He said sure and immediately flipped the book over to the back cover where he saw former NFL player Steve Largent's endorsement. He gave me a thumbs-up and cracked open the book to read.

About a half hour later, as we were preparing to land, Q.B. turned around and asked if we could talk as we walked to the baggage claim area. I looked at him with my toothpick arms and small stature, and feeling like I was just given a game-winning ball, I said sure.

As we walked and talked about how difficult the world is for teens today, we boarded the tram to take us to the main terminal. We stood on the train talking, and every so often Q.B. would slap me on the shoulder to highlight or accentuate some humorous or special point of our discussion about kids, marriage, family, and where we've made mistakes. Each slap sent me banging against the window of the tram.

As I was getting slapped around, I noticed a young man and his father standing next to us. The father asked if I would take a picture of him and his son, Mike, with Q.B. Happy to do so, I watched the father ask me a question in a happy voice and then bark out a harsh command to his son when we were ready to take the picture. "Don't screw this up, so smile," the dad said. As the tram was flying through the underground tunnel to the main terminal, Mike was trying to stand without holding on to a handrail. His dad barked at him again, "Quit being so tough and hold on," in a manner that was demeaning, demanding, and degrading. Then with another bark came a slap to Mike's back that was far different from the jovial slap that I was getting from the Hall of Famer.

My focus shifted from my conversation with Q.B. to the interaction between this father and son. With every move or comment Mike made, his dad corrected him, telling him to stand up straight, shake Q.B.'s hand, smile at the camera, don't close your eyes, quit being a dork, quit acting so tough, pull your pants back up. The verbal barrage went on and on and engrossed me so that I didn't even notice Q.B.'s jovial slaps, friendly words, and unforced laughter.

As we got off the tram and went up the escalator, I watched this dad continue to belittle his son, telling him how to step on the moving sidewalk, how to hold on to a handrail, and how to carry his luggage. This dad obviously thought he had a rebellious kid on his hands and was determined to correct him anytime he could. He looked at his son's behavior, labeled it as rebellious, and responded in a manner that would only cause more trouble.

I did not see a rebellious kid. I saw a normal 14-year-old kid. He was flapping his newfound wings, enjoying the new adventure of going to an NFL game for the first time, and not caring about everyone around him. He was a selfish kid, yes, because 14-year-old kids tend to be selfish. He didn't have a clue who Q.B. was, he thought that letting go of a handrail was no big deal, and he did not really care about having a picture with this great athlete.

I also saw a young man who was beginning to seethe with anger because of his father's well-intentioned physical slaps and verbal provocations. I saw a young man who was ready to blow like a volcano and spew his angry, hot, burning lava.

What the dad thought was a teen rebellion problem looked to me like a parental mishandling problem. Mike's dad wanted to handle his son's behavior, which he interpreted to be rebellious, by instructing him. But he was doing it in a way that only infuriated his son. Instead of squashing the "rebellion" (which was actually pretty normal behavior), Mike's dad was provoking actual rebellion in his son.

The problem was not necessarily the way Mike's dad handled what he was seeing. The problem is that Mike's dad didn't really *see* what his son was doing. This dad misinterpreted his son's actions and responded in a way that pushed Mike to the place Dad was trying to keep him away from. Here's the bottom line; parents are responsible to understand the actions of their children—much more than children are responsible to ensure that their parents interpret those actions correctly.

Without question, some teens are rebellious. Not all negative teen behaviors can be or should be justified or explained away. Some teens are irrational in their foolish pursuits, spiteful toward others, selfish in their thinking, and vengeful in their approach in order to make people angry. They intentionally buck authority. Their motivation is to cause problems any way they can. Those teens enjoy being miserable and making those around them miserable. They are rebellious. But there aren't as many of them as you might think.

Many teens are being mislabeled as rebellious because they display the same symptoms of inappropriate behavior as the truly rebellious teens. They appear rebellious, but they're really just responding to situations around them. The two are quite different, and the way parents interpret and handle each will determine whether they are successful at stopping the "rebellious" behavior. Parents must be able to delineate between the behaviors and mind-sets that are rebellious and those that are merely responding to the happenings in their world. If parents are unable to tell the difference, the parents' responses to the behavior might actually push their teen into full-blown rebellion.

Parents must see past the inappropriate behavior and straight into the heart of their teen. "What you see is what you get" doesn't hold water here. Scriptures say to look with the eyes of your heart (Ephesians 1:18). We are to examine the motives, not just the actions. If you look only at what you see, you might miss the intent behind your teen's actions and mistake it for something it is not.

Most parents just want inappropriate behavior to stop as soon as possible. But that behavior may be a helpful indicator—like a warning light on a dashboard—that tells you that something else is going on, something that has happened, is happening, or should happen. When that indicator light flashes on for the first time, parents do well to spend more time looking at the situation to pinpoint its cause and less time pointing a finger of blame.

> Do not judge, or you too will be judged. For in the same way you judge others, you will be judged, and with the measure you use, it will be measured to you.
>
> Why do you look at the speck of sawdust in your brother's eye and pay no attention to the plank in your own eye? How can you say to your brother, "Let me take the speck out of your eye," when all the time there is a plank in your own eye? You hypocrite, first take the plank out of your own eye, and then you will see clearly to remove the speck from your brother's eye (Matthew 7:1-5).

The message is simple. Be careful when you judge. Look at yourself as a possible cause of the problem. Pray that God would search your heart and see if you are parenting in ways that are hurtful. If you are, determine how your own habits affect your family and your teen. Find the root of your own stuff before digging into your kid's stuff, and you might find the cause of the problem. Take time to pull the plank out of your own eye so you can see clearly to remove the speck from your teen's eye. Then go help your son or daughter.

In many cases, the mere fact that you took time to look at yourself makes a huge difference in the life of your teen. Parents can be too quick to jump to their own conclusions about teen situations before they take time to look. Be slow to judge, slow to interpret, quick to listen, and willing to search for the reason behind the behavior. Only then will you be able to respond in a way that truly meets the needs of your teen, calms the atmosphere of your home, and prevents a greater storm from forming.

When is your teen's behavior a sign of true rebellion, and when is it not? I can't answer that for you because your situation is unique.

But I will tell you this: Kids' behavior is often much more response than it is rebellion. And I say that to you with a slap on the shoulder from my toothpick arms.

After that meeting with Q.B. and the first night of our parenting seminar, Jan and I went to our hotel dead tired from answering questions about teens and struggles. As we climbed into bed, I turned on the TV to watch Jay Leno and the *Tonight Show*. Guess who was one of the guests that night? A large 60-year-old man—this time with no baseball cap. I massaged my sore shoulder and chuckled while I watched, thinking, *You just can't judge a book by its cover.*

Chapter 2

The Three Amigos

■ ■ ■ ■

Megan, Jayme, and Whitney arrived at our Heartlight residential program for teens and soon became inseparable, earning the title the Three Amigos. Heartlight's ministry includes a national radio show that gives parents insight into the lives of teens who seem to be spinning out of control. I was working on the radio show from Nashville, preparing to interview the Three Amigos.

As the interviewer, I asked each of the girls what led to their move to Heartlight, what their home environment was like, and what advice they would give parents to help keep their child from ending up in the same place. These are typical questions we ask teens on every show, and I assumed we would get typical answers. Not that day. What we heard was powerful and poignant.

Megan got on the phone first. She began to tell me all the things that she had been doing wrong. I was a little amazed that a girl that I hadn't even met yet was so open in her discussion. I casually asked her when she thought her struggles began. Her reply startled me. She said, "My dad died of cancer two years ago, and it was really hard. It was hard because I hadn't seen him in a while, and when he died, I knew that I would never see him again or have the relationship I always wanted."

I teared up as she poured out her heart and continued to share her and her mother's struggles. I wanted to hug her through the phone as

I heard the longing in her voice to have a dad. Father's Day was just a few days away, and I knew this little girl was going to wake up on that day and feel the loss all over again. Those thoughts tore me up, and quite honestly, I was glad when the interview was over.

Next on the docket was Jayme. I met Jayme's mother the day they arrived at Heartlight, but I had not yet met Jayme. As she started to talk about her inappropriate behaviors and out-of-control lifestyle, we asked her how she thought it all got started. Out of the blue, Jayme said, "It all started to unravel when my dad was murdered."

I looked at my co-host in disbelief as I tried not to act overly surprised or emotional during the recording. As Jayme continued to share her insights about how she had struggled through her life, every one of us in the studio realized that this Father's Day needed to be different for our kids.

Finally, Whitney came on the phone. She was the last of the three to arrive at Heartlight, and because I had been traveling, my first introduction to her was over that phone call. As we talked and shared about life at home, she began to tell our listeners when all the problems began. "When I was ten years old, our family was on our way to get me a puppy a few days before Thanksgiving. All of a sudden, our car was upside-down. My sister and I were in the backseat, and I knew that my mom and dad were dead. A semitrailer truck had smashed into our car, and life would never be the same. After the accident, we went to live with my aunt and uncle."

My jaw was on the floor. All three girls, picked randomly from all the kids at Heartlight, had lost someone dear in their lives. It was moving, to say the least. As the Three Amigos revealed their hearts, we all felt an overwhelming sense of compassion toward these girls. I had always been told that there is no motion without emotion. Well, we had plenty of motion in that recording studio that day. Each one of us would have jumped through that phone line, hugged each of the girls, and pledged our lives to help them through their struggle if we could.

When teens suffer through tragedies like these, we can understand why they might seem to spin out of control with unacceptable and inappropriate behaviors. Their difficulty during adolescence is easier to understand because of the way they've suffered. Their bad behavior is easier to accept. Many parents look for an incident in their teen's life that could justify their child's choices. In their search to pinpoint the cause of their teen's demise, some parents overturn every possible rock to find the incident that would explain the baffling behavior. Counselors do this all the time. Their job is to look at a person's history and discover how certain thinking patterns were formed and why particular behaviors are displayed.

Wouldn't it be easier to understand your daughter's depression if you found out that she had been raped on a date the year before? Wouldn't it be easier to accept your next-door-neighbor's son's outbursts of anger if you knew that he was struggling with the suicide of his father? Wouldn't it be easier to explain to your friends why your teen is dropping out of school if they knew that he had been sexually and physically abused by a stepfather? Wouldn't it be easier to tolerate your child's disrespect and disobedience if you knew that the death of a classmate had rocked her world and that she was struggling through feelings of significant loss?

Sure it would. Pinpointing the cause of the struggle helps anyone better understand the situation, accept the behaviors more, and explain them to family and friends. Pinpointing helps parents eliminate the chance that their teen could possibly be *choosing* a lifestyle that is so foreign to their family values and their desires for their teen.

Many parents are scared to death to admit that their teen might have actually chosen a path of destruction, so they spend years trying to find that one reason that justifies their teen's waywardness. They just can't believe that anyone in his right mind would choose to do what their child did, so they continue the search for a diagnosis, an incident, a victimization, or an excuse.

But be careful! When the bad behavior has no clear cause, this search only encourages teens' irresponsibility and further enables their lack of ownership for the path they have chosen. Sometimes teens may have no real reason to act the way they do. They simply made some bad choices.

When parents can't identify a cause, they can easily lose any sense of compassion for their teen. They are no longer moved the way we in the radio station were moved toward Megan, Jayme, and Whitney. In fact, when kids have no apparent reason for their rebellion, parents have plenty of emotions that cause them to want to move their hearts away from their teen. They are more likely to give their teens a slug than to give them a hug. When teens' rebellion rests solely on their choices, parents have a harder time understanding, accepting, explaining, and tolerating the behavior. This usually moves parents to anger—the typical emotional response for not getting what they want for their child.

In anger, judgment sets in. Bitterness invades a once-beautiful relationship. Disillusionment replaces trust, love is withdrawn, and tears flow. Dreams fade, and successes are questioned. Innocent comments are interpreted negatively. Relationships are challenged, and families are destroyed. Teens begin to feel that they are loved only when they make good choices, not when they make poor ones, so their relationship with their parents seems to be conditional. This moves them even further away from mom and dad and closer to anyone whom they say "loves me as I am." Emotional distance increases, communication falters, and another great relationship's demise is chalked up to teen rebellion.

Parents, let me ask you a question: If you've trusted God with your child during the good times, why is it hard to trust Him with your teen during the hard times?

You may not find a gut-wrenching story behind your teen's demise that would motivate you to do whatever it takes to help your child work through difficult times. But that doesn't mean your child is no less worthy to receive your compassion, grace, love, acceptance, and involvement.

Parents tend to feel that because children chose a particular path, they must now pay the consequences. Of course, I do believe that sin has consequences. Foolishness has consequences as well. And I believe that a teen will reap what he sows. I strongly believe that teens should spend the night in jail, pay their own fines, suffer consequences for irresponsibility, and learn the hard way for their immaturity. But I just as strongly believe that the threat of losing a relationship with their parents should not be a bargaining tool to get them to turn from their wicked ways. The wages of sin is death, but even death will never separate us from God our Father. Similarly, nothing should separate us from our children.

This love of God, who has promised to never leave (to move away from) us or forsake (abandon, desert, or renounce) us, is difficult to live out when a child is making bad decisions. The commitment can tear your heart out. But it is necessary if we indeed love our children even when they fail or make poor choices.

So what's the point of the Three Amigos' stories? What if your teen hasn't faced tragedy of that magnitude or anything else you can put your finger on to cause him to turn from you like he has? The bottom line is this: God is engaged in our lives even if we don't have an emotional, tearful story, and He isn't pushed away by our boring ballad of poor choices and rebellious antics. If we are to love our kids as God has loved us, our involvement with our kids should be like His. I've heard thousands of tear-jerking stories. And I've heard just as many stories of teens who made horrendous mistakes and foolish choices. I've come to the conclusion that the emotion or lack of emotion a struggling teen's personal story stirs in others' hearts should not validate or invalidate that teen's need for help. Nor should it determine how involved a person is in her life. Here are four lessons I have learned through the years:

1. Most behavior has a root cause. A story may not be as moving as any one of the Three Amigos', but that doesn't mean we should ignore it. Some roots are shocking, and some roots are commonplace. Some run deep, and others are shallow. You may not see them, but that doesn't mean they're not there. Dig for them.

2. Abnormal behavior usually begins with an abnormal circumstance. Death, divorce, being bullied, failing for the first time, feeling like an outcast—all of these, to an adolescent, can be extremely painful and feel abnormal.

3. Every behavior has a motivating factor. Teens strive to get something out of everything they do. It's their nature, the way they are wired. Quite honestly, something would be wrong if it wasn't this way.

4. If you believe that a teen should be able to make choices, then you should be prepared for them to make some poor ones.

So, how are the Three Amigos?

Honestly, Megan is not doing so well. She's learning that the tragedy she's clung to for so many years doesn't give her license for continued inappropriate behavior. She's finding that old habits are hard to break and that the tears people shed for her now are not for her sad story but for the sad way she is using her story to justify her actions.

Jayme is doing well. Her dad's murder will always be a part of her story, but it isn't all of the story. Her willingness to deal with the deeper issues surrounding the absence of a dad in her life has moved her to a much healthier place. This young lady has learned that tragedy can point the way to greater things.

Whitney still struggles. She is a tenderhearted young lady to whom I hope to bring a puppy one day. Confronting loss and tragedy is a long process. Healing hurts and disappointments can take even longer. I long for the day when I can sit at her wedding and celebrate God's faithfulness and commitment to her.

Who is your Megan, your Jayme, your Whitney? Teens' personal tragedies or root causes may seem small to you, but to them, they may be huge. The way you love them and stick by them today may determine your relationship—and their behavior—tomorrow.

Chapter 3

Iceberg or Ice Cube?

■ ■ ■ ■

I remember the first time I cursed out loud.

On a hot, humid day, the buzz of mosquitoes passed back and forth in front of my ears as my friends and I boiled crawdads at the clubhouse in the woods next to our homes in New Orleans. We carefully tied pieces of bacon on the end of our fishing lines and gently lowered the bait into one of the many canals surrounding our neighborhood. When we felt a little tug, we gently raised our meal as it remained clamped onto the bacon. Six boys with six poles. We caught about a hundred crawdads and then put them into a pot of boiling spices. Man, were we living!

After a crawdad meal that was more work than it was filling, we decided to have our daily game of war in the snake-infested wooded area that we thought we owned. Running and screaming while shooting our plastic guns and throwing our homemade wooden grenades at each other, we reenacted battles we heard about on the evening news or through the war stories of our fathers. My "unit" decided to hide in a drainage pipe just big enough to squeeze into. Our plan was for all three of us to scoot into the drainage pipe and then jump out and ambush the enemy unit as it approached. I backed in first and kept backing until all three of us were in. I hadn't planned on not being able to get out the other end.

I was ten feet into the pipe and could see only the soles of the muddy shoes on my friend in front of me. The farther I scooted back, the darker it got dark. The darker it became, the more scared I was. I gently asked the fellow in front of me to let me out. It didn't work. Either he didn't hear me or was so consumed with our mission that he didn't pay attention. I started to scream at my unit to get out. I could barely hear the guy in the front whisper, "It's not time." I thought otherwise.

As I felt my shoulders press against that concrete tube, I screamed that it *was* time. When all my normal attempts didn't work, I switched to desperate tactics. I exploded and began pushing until my actions spoke louder than my words, and my friend in front of me started yelling for the one in front of him to get out. I screamed louder and louder, and when all I knew to do wasn't working fast enough, I resorted to cussing, crying, and pushing more and more. I became frantic and out of control. I was claustrophobic and squeezed, and I was going to do whatever my little ten-year-old body had to do to get freedom.

I came out of the end of that pipe cursing at my best friends, screaming every naughty word I'd ever read on bathroom walls or seen painted in graffiti on concrete drainage canals. I was hitting my friends with my plastic gun, screaming at them at the top of my lungs, and crying uncontrollably in the process. Nobody around me knew what to do, and neither did I. I had never experienced claustrophobia. I remember to this day the feeling I experienced when my fear left me as I breathed in fresh humid air, saw that I was okay, and realized I had regained my freedom. There have been other times in my life when I have had the same feelings and have exploded with the same reactions.

When I was 11, I was working out with the swim team when a couple of older guys had fun with the little kid and held me underwater as a joke. When I fought my way to the surface, I punched one in the face and told the other that I was going to kill him—in a voice that even I didn't recognize as my own. At 12 I played football with a group of guys who decided to pile on the little kid with chicken legs. I remember trying to keep my wits as I lay pressured, unable to move, and constricted. When my friends ignored my pleas to let me up, I exploded with adrenaline-fueled strength and started biting, kicking, and screaming...anything I could do to get freedom. People saw a side of me they had never seen before. No one thought that Chicken Legs had it in him to take on a group of guys who were just joking around.

My friends' parents who saw me during one of my "fight for freedom" episodes thought I was rebellious and out of control. They didn't let their kids hang around this angry kid. They felt sorry for my parents, who had to live with such an out-of-control child. But what these parents saw as an iceberg was nothing more than a small ice cube. My actions weren't indicative of a massive behavioral problem; instead, they were isolated to one kind of incident—I simply couldn't stand being hemmed in or pinned down. It was not as big of a deal as it appeared. Once I got air, saw the light of day, or wasn't constricted or restricted, everything was fine. My behavior was normal.

Many parents look at the actions and behaviors of their teens and think they're dealing with an overwhelmingly big, dangerous iceberg. They see their teens suddenly become defiant, rebellious, and angry. They watch their teens' disrespect grow, their vocabulary rot, and their demeanor sour. Parents fear that a relationship that was once vibrant and warm is growing into a mountain of ice. Behavior deteriorates, and the fight is on. When parents try to correct their teens' behavior by enforcing more rules and consequences, their children's actions spin more and more out of hand.

This type of scenario is all too common. I hear about it daily from parents who want to know what to do about a child whose relationship with them has suddenly turned cold. Parents want to know how big a problem they're dealing with and how to melt the iceberg. They want to know what to do, but I often direct their attention to what they need *not* to do.

Let me explain.

Many parents are well-intentioned when they provide much for their children. They want so many good things for their teens that they remain overly active in their teens' lives to ensure their children's accomplishment. Somewhere in the midst of all that providing, parents sometimes forget to train their children to thrive on their own. Many parents have wonderful relationships with their young kids but hover way too long in their children's development, thinking they can teach their children better than others can.

But "helicopter" parents become not only a distraction, but even an annoyance and a barricade to their teens' growth and development into young adults. Parents sometimes give too much and don't allow the teens to develop their own drive to succeed. Doing everything for teens isn't a good thing. Kids moving through adolescence should be given more and more freedom so they can become more and more independent. A man is eventually to leave his mother. A woman is to eventually leave her home. A young man should be able to take care of himself. Teens must become independent. Even a mother bird with a brain that weighs less than an ounce knows she must do two things: kick her babies out of the nest (quit providing) and make sure they know how to fly (train them to survive and succeed).

Parents and teens agree that teens need to become independent. The rub lies in the fact that teens want their freedom too quickly, and parents are often hesitant and slow to give it.

I met with a 16-year-old named Nick. He was a good kid, but for whatever reason, he was acting out toward his mom and dad. Mom said that he would cuss at them, didn't want to be with them, avoided opportunities to share time with his family, and spent time alone. He was becoming disrespectful, disobedient, and dishonest in his pursuit of freedom. This was a young man who had grown up in the church, seemed to get along with everyone except the people in his home, and did well in school. But the minute he walked in the door, the fight began. To combat his negativity, his parents established new rules and enforced consequences to curb his anger and disrespect. Whenever they took away privileges, he became almost violent and began cursing and screaming, telling his mom and dad they were destroying his life. Everything they were doing wasn't working, and trying to enforce anything was like throwing gasoline on a fire. His parents were at their wits' end.

As I spent time with Nick, I found he had some pretty neat things going for him. He wanted to work at a job. He wanted to make money. He wanted to make his own decisions. He longed for the opportunity to make some choices and fulfill his plans. He loved church. He said he loved his parents but that they were driving him nuts.

He was frustrated that his mother was still buying his clothes. She was still taking him to school in the morning and picking him up in the afternoon. They woke him up every morning and made him eat breakfast with his little sisters. His parents told him when to get his hair cut and what it was to look like. They restricted his music to only Christian music, picked the friends he was to be with, and kept him from those he was not to be with. He wasn't allowed to date until his senior year, and most of his discussions with his parents centered around academics. Nick's parents wanted him not to work so he could focus on school. Nick stated that whenever he wanted to do something alone, his parents intruded and tried to participate. In short, Nick felt as if his parents were treating him like a little kid. These were his exact words: "They're smothering me and keeping me from where I want to be."

Nick's reactions and responses to his parents' good intentions were inappropriate, but his motivation was certainly appropriate. He too was claustrophobic, and he was showing his desperation to break free from constraints that were inappropriate for a young man his age. They were well-intentioned but a little too tight.

This happens to many families, and it may be happening in yours. Parents' hesitancy to grant freedom in a timely manner and their inability to see their children's need for more freedom can push their teens into the emotional equivalent of the drain pipe I felt trapped in. Teens can feel as if they are being held underwater for too long. When Nick made appropriate attempts to discuss these issues or talk about his frustrations, his parents either didn't listen or didn't seriously consider what he said. When appropriate means of resolution don't work, teens usually move to the inappropriate. Nick made that move, and his parents were caught by surprise.

Bad behavior is never appropriate, and doing wrong is never okay—even with the right motivation. Nick was wrong in the way he was handling the situation, but he was well-intentioned. His parents were wrong in the way they were handling their son, but they were well-intentioned too. The challenge in this kind of situation is to figure out how to make two wrongs right.

Some parents tell me they have to do all these things for their children, to limit and restrict the kids' activities because they are just too irresponsible. If this is what you find yourself saying, let me ask you a question: Which comes first? A teen who is irresponsible or parents who didn't allow their child to make decisions and fail?

It doesn't really matter at this point, does it? Here's a more important question: How can you give your teen the responsibility she needs for her life, coupled with the freedom to live in such a way that she can develop a sense of independence and maturity?

Most parents feel awkward giving freedom to children who have tried to obtain that freedom inappropriately. That's understandable. But let me interject another important word here: *grace*. Grace is getting something one doesn't deserve. Nick doesn't deserve freedom, does he? Not with the way he's been acting. But the fact that he doesn't deserve it doesn't mean that he shouldn't get it. That's real grace. And grace at this point would give him the freedom to undo what he and his parents have done wrong.

Grace usually gives a fresh start. Most relationships that are spinning out of control need to start over again. Remember, what appears to be an iceberg may only be an ice cube. That was the case with Nick's family. And it may be the same for yours.

How can you tell? I encouraged Nick's family to walk through this process to help them change the way they operate and to keep Nick from needing to kick and scream to get his message across.

Recognize the Squeeze

Squeeze anything hard enough and it will explode. Some teens don't mind a tight structure and are comfortable with Mom and Dad doing most things for them. But some people are claustrophobic. They will desire freedom, want independence, and try to break free from Mom and Dad.

If you really want to know if you are squeezing your teen too tight, ask a trusted friend to spend an hour with you. Tell her what you require of your child and what you do with him, and talk about the nature of your child. Remember, many parents hold the reins a little too tight.

Release Your Grip

Sit down with your teen and share ways that you can give him more freedom. He'll welcome this, and you will be able to share your concerns about his newfound freedom. If you just can't give up some areas right now, tell him you want to work on some areas first. Be sure to inform him how you're going to prepare him to be ready to accept the new freedom and corresponding responsibilities.

During this process, remember the word *grace*. It might not feel right. I've found that if grace feels good, it probably isn't grace. Grace is needed most when it is undeserved.

Restore the Relationship

The warm waters of your inviting relationship can melt an ice cube in no time. The simplest way to begin the conversation of restoration is to admit where you have been wrong. Period. Tell your teen where you've made mistakes, where you haven't allowed her to grow up, where you have kept her from maturing, and how you'd like to relate differently in the future. Sharing your failures just might give her the motivation and example she needs to do the same. Usually, an admission includes two simple words: *I'm sorry*.

This process of recognizing, releasing, and restoring sets you up to move to the fourth step.

Require Responsibility

When a parent limits a teen by not giving him freedom in a timely manner, the parent usually withholds responsibility too. If you're going to give the freedom, you must give the responsibility as well. You have acknowledged your mistake in the relationship and have acted on that by giving more freedom, so you now have the opportunity to require something from your teen—responsibility. How do you do that? Let me give you some examples:

- "Son, you're right. You're sixteen and should be able to drive yourself to school. I'm going to let you do that, but you'll need to pay for the gas you use."

- "You can listen to other music than what we've allowed, but please be sensitive and play it on your headphones or iPod."

- "You're right about us reading your text messages. We won't do that any longer, but we need you to start paying for the phone."

- "You're right about the jokes…they'll quit."

- "You're right about eating breakfast with your sisters. Eat when you want, but make sure you clean up after yourself."

- "We're going to put some money in a checking account in your name. The amount will take care of what we would have spent on clothes, haircuts, lunch money, school needs, and gas. We'll deposit money at the beginning of the month, and your responsibility is to make sure it lasts the whole month. We won't add more if you run out before the next month."

While you're at it, add a couple like this:

- "Come to think of it, Mom's feeling a little overworked, and she thinks you ought to do your own laundry."

- "Since you'll be driving to school, could you take your younger sisters to school every morning? We'll pick them up. That will be a big help to your mom."

Requiring some responsibility from your teen will help her correlate responsibility with freedom and overcome her sense of entitlement. It also helps prepare her for the world in which she will eventually live. The more responsibility you take on for your teen, the less responsibility she will assume for her own life. As parents give teens responsibility, the teens' maturity develops.

They want it. Give it to them. You'll be surprised at the way your teen feels coming out of that drainage pipe, or out from under the water, or out from under all that has been piled on him. And you'll find that your response is different as well.

Chapter 4

Mad at Mom or Dad with Nowhere to Go

■ ■ ■ ■

Most of us adults have the luxury of being able to walk away from situations or people who cause conflict in our lives or make us angry. We can walk out after poor wait service in a restaurant, or we can leave a spouse. (This is not recommended, but it is our choice.) Adults can eliminate people in their lives at work by firing them, by quitting the job, or moving to another city. If a conflict at church won't go away, adults can change churches, cancel memberships, or just quit attending. Many situations are inevitable and beyond any person's control, but still, most adults usually have the ability and luxury to get away from whatever makes them mad.

Teens can enjoy this luxury in some arenas of their life, but not in two of the most important places: at home and at school. This chapter will focus on the home front. For the most part, teens are a captive audience and can't get away from family members who offend them or cause problems for them, whether deserved or undeserved.

Of course, something is very good about having to work through issues and difficulties with family members. No doubt, just as iron sharpens iron, one family member does sharpen another. I've always stated that a commitment to remain engaged with one another while one struggles or hurts the other is necessary if that relationship is to deepen.

But parents can make mistakes, and like large stones thrown into a pond, their actions have consequences that ripple out and affect their children. Teens' anger is often the effect of those ripples.

Teen rebellion is sometimes nothing more than a response to unresolved issues caused by parents' actions. And whether the resolution occurs in fifteen minutes or ten years, that anger can be the root of much of the inappropriate, reactionary behavior in a teen's life. Proverbs 29:22 tells us, "An angry man stirs up dissension, and a hot-tempered one commits many sins," and Ephesians 4:26 warns us, "In your anger do not sin." Being angry about situations and about relationships with people is okay. Allowing that anger to cause you to sin is not okay.

The key to changing a teen's unacceptable behavior is to get to the root of the anger. Calm the ripples before they affect all areas of his life. People who are angry begin to act on that anger and cause more problems for themselves and those around them.

Parents must honestly and humbly consider that the root of their teens' issue may be that Mom or Dad (or both) made some serious mistakes, and they must assume responsibility for the effect their actions are having on their teens. A mother's and father's sin never give license to a teen to act inappropriately or give justification for her sin. But neither does the sin of a teen give justification to parents to ignore the part they might have played in causing the situation.

Many times I see teens who want payback for their parents' mistakes. Many want to let their parents know how much hurt and damage they have caused. Many want vengeance. Many are angry that they have been violated and are forced to live with the person who has violated them, eat with him every night, interact with him, and act as though nothing has happened.

Adults can get away from people who have violated them or damaged them; teens don't have that luxury. Instead, they resort to "fight or flight." In chapter 3, we saw that Nick chose to fight. What about your teen?

When parents don't understand how their actions affect their teen, and the teen doesn't know how to process the hurt she feels, the stage is set for a good brawl. The teen usually intends to inflict pain on those who hurt her and to communicate the hateful, hurtful message that someone must pay for the burden she must carry.

Here are some other examples.

Linda chose to avoid her dad and cut off their relationship when he gambled away all the family money—including her college fund. She became hateful and mean. She wanted her dad to pay for how he had violated her, her mother, and their family. Her parents' divorce wasn't enough to convey the pain she felt, so this sweet girl—who had made straight A's in school, was the head of the cheerleading squad, and was ready to enter her senior year—trashed her grades, quit the cheerleading squad, and threatened to not graduate, just to send a message to her dad that he had messed things up. Linda chose to fight. Regardless of the consequences and groundings she suffered for bad grades, she dug in her heels and was bound and determined to make her dad pay and realize how much she had been hurt. She wasn't rebelling; she was seeking revenge.

Blake exerted power over his dad after his dad was convicted of child molestation and was labeled as a sex offender. Blake decided he didn't have to listen to the rules his dad established, and he roamed the country and did as he pleased. Blake was embarrassed in front of his friends and ridiculed by others, and other parents wouldn't allow their kids to come over to his house. Blake boiled with anger and occasionally exploded on people, on other people's property, and on his dad. Dad didn't know what to do, so everything in the family started to spin out of control. Whenever Dad tried to restore order in the family, Blake's actions shouted, "What gives you the right to correct us and tell us what to do?"

When Whitney's mother's addiction to pain pills became public, Whitney chose to distance herself from her mother (who led the women's Bible studies at church) through seductive dress and anything that could hurt her mother. On weekends, she drowned her embarrassment with alcohol, partying, clubbing, and sex. When she got pregnant, she didn't think twice about blaming it on her mother, reminding her that she was the cause of Whitney's demise. Weird way of thinking, isn't it? Whitney wasn't rebelling; she was bitter.

When Carl's dad was sent to prison for embezzling from his oil company, Carl didn't know what life was going to be like for the next five years without Dad around. They had been best friends, and now his best friend would be absent all of his high school years. Shame, embarrassment, ridicule, and loneliness moved Carl to isolate himself from his normal social world. Visiting his dad eventually became too painful, knowing his dad wasn't going to be home for so many more years. After four years of isolation, the only things Carl enjoyed were skateboarding and hanging out with friends. His new social circle led him to increasingly unacceptable behaviors. Carl was in his own kind of prison. He didn't know how to get out of his pain, so he chose to live life in another world. He neglected his family, his values, and the things he once enjoyed doing with his dad. Carl wasn't rebellious; he was just trying to keep his head above water, fearful that he was drowning in the loss of his dad.

When Jessica heard of her mother's affair with the high school principal, Jessica adopted an I-don't-care attitude that poisoned her interactions with friends, school, God, and her church. She spun out of control and found a new set of friends who didn't know her mom and didn't care if they did. She was National Honor Society president, but that didn't matter because she didn't care. She wasn't rebelling; she was merely deflecting the hurt and disappointment she felt.

When people began to hear about Chip's dad's affair with the mother of one of his middle-school friends and her subsequent pregnancy, Chip lashed out in anger. As his friends' opinion of his dad deteriorated, Chip began defending his dad by picking fights. He began to feel that the new baby was more important than he was, that his mother was consumed with her own grief over losing a husband, and that his dad was so busy with both that he didn't have time for Chip. Chip felt as if he had lost his mother and father. But he soon found that smoking marijuana made him feel good when he was feeling so bad. He wasn't rebelling; he was grieving the loss of a mother, father, and his family.

Kerri was the perfect kid. She loved church, was involved in mission projects, was adored by her brothers, and stayed away from sex, drugs, and alcohol. Her parents allowed their stunning daughter to date at age 16. On her first date, the guy tried to go too far, and Kerri was shocked and stunned by the encounter. Her parents asked about the date, and she shared what had happened. Kerri's father, in the heat of the moment, said that Kerri should have done something different, was incompetent not to fend off his advances, and probably asked for it by the way she was dressed. Whether her father had any factual points correct or not, his words verbally crucified his daughter. Kerri stated that what this boy did made her want to commit suicide. Her dad said she didn't have the guts to do it. Feeling devalued and misunderstood, Kerri decided to show her dad how gutsy she really was. She got into her parents' medicine cabinet and took 30 sleeping pills.

Kerri's parents had no idea what the fight had done to their daughter until dad came upstairs to apologize, found Kerri asleep, and couldn't wake her. Kerri awoke a few hours later after being rushed to the emergency room and having her stomach pumped. Kerri wasn't rebellious; she was sending her dad a message. If she showed her dad that he was wrong about her being too afraid to kill herself, she could prove he was also wrong about the way she handled her date.

Am I giving permission to teens to act out the way they do when parents have wronged them? Absolutely not! All parents have made mistakes with their children, even the man in one of my seminars who explained that he believed in the old school of parenting and that he had never been wrong. He believed that as a parent he's always right and that his daughter needed to understand that and show some respect.

"May I ask you a question?" I asked. He nodded yes. I asked him, "Why are you at this seminar?" He explained that his daughter was causing some problems and that he just needed a little help with her because she was just not acting right. I didn't comment on that; I just stated what I still believe today—that when people think they're always right, they'll soon be proven wrong. It was sooner rather than later for this father.

The intentional behaviors I've described above are responses of situations and not unprovoked rebellious behaviors intent on causing pain or damage. Kids practice these behaviors because parents miss the fact that their actions are a part of the issue, or they don't remedy the situation in a correct and effective way.

This is an important concept to understand. Most parents, when seeing out-of-control behavior by their teens, set restrictions, pull privileges, administer consequences, and punish. This only inflames the situation. The teens already feel hurt by their parent, they can't get out of the situation, and they feel as if the situation and conflict either can't or won't be resolved. Then the parents add the fuel of consequences to the raging fire already burning out of control. Piling on more consequences in these situations is just like adding gasoline. An explosion will result and someone will get hurt.

Parents who are part of the cause of their teens' behaviors will see their teens' anger turn into frustration and then bitterness. If the anger is not resolved or talked out, the teens will begin to act it out. These teens may desire vengeance and isolation. Parents must accept responsibility for the damage they have done in the life of their teens and seek reconciliation. In this way, they can stop feeding the fire and eventually snuff it out altogether.

What can you do if you realize this is your situation? Let me give you some ideas.

The first step is to realize you might have something to do with your teen's struggle. Simply understanding your mistakes and their ripple effect has an amazing way of tempering your response to your child. I reiterate: This doesn't mean your child's out-of-control behavior is ever justified or acceptable. But when you understand your involvement in the demise of your teen's mind-set and corresponding behavior, you will naturally move toward him with compassion, empathy, and a desire to ask for forgiveness.

How you approach your teen about his unacceptable behavior will make all the difference in his response to you. He will be much more likely to admit his guilt if you admit yours. He will accept more responsibility for his actions if you will accept responsibility for yours. And he is more likely to lovingly respond to your admission of guilt and accept your apologies if you lovingly engage with him.

In golfing terms, your approach in your swing will determine how well you hit the ball. In horse terms, the way you sit in the saddle will determine how well the horse responds to your commands. In swimming terms, the smoothness of your stroke will determine the length of your swim. Approach is everything. The demeanor of your approach will determine the demeanor of your teen's response.

How do you approach your teen? With gentleness and humility. On your knees, Dad. On your knees, Mom. Admitting fault. Accepting *your* mistakes. Understanding her response. And asking her forgiveness. I've always said that forgiveness is giving up hope that you'll ever have a better past. You're not asking her to just get over it or forget about what you've done. And you certainly don't want to make the mistake of giving excuses for why you did what you did. That will only escalate an already volatile situation. Approach her in a way that reflects what you truly feel for her. Your humbleness and gentleness will set the stage for this meeting and any upcoming meetings with her.

When parents admit failure but then make excuses, they usually end up with more problems than solutions. Teens will simply add *denial* to the list of wrongs that have caused them pain. It's just one more ripple effect of your actions. Limit your initial conversation to simply admitting that you have messed up and identifying the problems your mistakes have made. That initial conversation should be flavored with phrases like these:

- "I made a mistake."
- "I hurt you."
- "I never thought that what I was doing would hurt you...
  because I never thought."

- "I caused this problem."

- "I was wrong."

Explaining the reasoning behind your actions is not helpful in this conversation. Your intent should be to admit fault and ask forgiveness—period. Don't make excuses, reason your actions away, or justify your behavior. If you do, that is what your teen will do at your next conversation.

In the second meeting, begin the conversation by asking your teen if she has any questions about what you discussed with her before. This shows that you care about what she thinks and feels. If she accuses you, consider admitting guilt even if you don't fully agree with her. This prevents arguments and helps you to move on.

The next step in your second conversation is to share your concerns about some of her behaviors, fully understanding that your actions helped motivate those behaviors. State your disagreement with the behaviors you see regardless of how much you may have contributed. You may say something like this:

- "I know that your mom and my divorce caused problems in your life and has been hard, but I cannot allow your behavior to continue. My wrong does not justify your behavior, even though it may have caused it."

- "I was wrong in my actions, but my actions cannot give license to your actions that are just as wrong. I can't allow that to happen any longer."

- "I almost lost you when I did wrong...I'm not going to lose you because you're doing wrong."

- "I'm paying the price for my mistakes. I don't want you to have to pay that same price, so I will not allow the behaviors I see to continue...no matter what I have to do to stop this downward spiral."

- "I didn't think about you when I did wrong, but I'm thinking about you now when you're doing wrong, and I don't want my wrong actions to ruin your life, as they have mine."

Can you hear the flavor of these statements? They convey your responsibility for your mistakes and a commitment not to allow your child to use your mistakes as the jumping off point for his own downfall. It's a loving and graceful message: "I made mistakes, but that doesn't mean you have license now to do what you want and ignore my directions, rules, and boundaries."

In this conversation, you should convey to your teen what you're willing to do and let him know the options that exist to remedy the behavior and underlying issues. This may be as simple as talking through issues one-on-one or as challenging as making the decision to send your child to a place where he can get the help and protection he needs.

These are tough conversations. It's hard to admit when you're wrong. But think about it—your teen knows it anyway. The real issue is whether you're able to admit it and restore a relationship with a child who was put into your life for a reason, regardless of the mistakes you've made. The way you work through these issues may present an opportunity to share with your daughter how to respond in the future when she makes similar mistakes with her own children.

Of course, if you committed a mistake and admitted it was wrong but then continue in your wrong behavior, you don't have a leg to stand on when you ask your teen to stop his corresponding and responsive behavior. For example, consider a parent who apologizes for the effect drinking has had on the family but then pours a glass of wine with dinner, saying it's no big deal. To your teen, your continued bad behavior justifies his continued bad behavior. When you make this kind of choice, you're telling your teen that you don't mind putting him in continuous and ongoing pain for your own selfish desires. I have no words of wisdom for you if you are not willing to change. If you won't, why should your child?

My son, Adam, went through a divorce a few years ago. In all my discussions with him, I pleaded with him to think through what he was doing. Recently, he told me that when he dropped the first stone and filed for divorce, he thought he understood all the ramifications of divorce. But he admits now that he didn't have any idea how much the ripples of his actions would affect his life. Very few people going through a divorce consider the effects their young children will face as they grow up. Please don't feel that I'm picking on anyone who has been divorced, but I've seen the effects of divorce on kids, and the ripples are huge. Not many hurting adults who want to get out of their marriage realize how hard it will be for their children to grow up with a single mom or dad, deal with the absence of a parent, handle having stepparents, or split time between homes. All of these things have an effect on kids.

I'm not passing judgment, but I want us to understand that when we do something that negatively affects our teens, we must approach them in a way that admits fault, seeks forgiveness, and restores a relationship where damage has been done.

Chapter 5

The Homeschool Rebel

■ ■ ■ ■

People always ask me about the teens we have at our Heartlight residential facility in Texas. They are shocked when I tell them that the kids who come to live with us are great kids from great families. They just need some help because their lives are spinning out of control. Most are in desperate situations that demand drastic measures. Many are homeschooled kids who have moved into adolescence and are having major struggles—major enough that they have to leave home and move into a residential counseling or treatment center just to survive. That's pretty severe.

I don't say that with any malice or judgment. It's just a fact. More than one-third of the young people who have lived with us were homeschooled a significant number of years, and they hit a brick wall when they tried to enter a normal social environment. This doesn't mean that homeschooling is wrong, nor does it mean that the parents were misdirected. It doesn't even mean that what a child learned educationally and relationally was not worthwhile. Most teens struggle. But many of the ones we see are kids who have been homeschooled.

I'm not talking about a young kid raised in a little house on the prairie who is then sent to an inner-city high school in Los Angeles and is having a difficult time adjusting to his new environment. I'm talking about a great kid, raised in a good home, with great parents, who is struggling.

To ignore the problems a lot of homeschool kids experience would be foolish. To ignore the fact that many homeschooled teens have difficulty integrating into a normal social environment would be to miss the opportunity to help them get back on track with their lives and families.

Homeschooling is a controversial issue for some. Whenever I mention homeschool on the radio, I get calls from people who misinterpret my comments as criticism of a wonderful opportunity. Every article I write about homeschooling is countered with the criticism that I never homeschooled my kids. If I'm speaking at an event, more times than not when approached by a believer in homeschooling, I'm ridiculed for my comments about struggling homeschoolers. So may I just suggest that we all put our weapons down?

I'm not on the hunt for new reasons why teens spin out of control. This chapter is addressed to parents who have lovingly given more of their life to their kids than most parents give, and my intent is to help them get control of an out-of-control mess. Remember, we're looking for reasons why teens act out the way they do so we can find answers and directives that will save their lives and families.

I look for reasons behind a teen's behavior. I look at behaviors, talk with the parents and the child, and try to determine what the driving motivation behind a teen's actions might be. I've found a common thread with these homeschooled teens. (The problems don't usually show themselves until a child reaches adolescence, when the combined forces of social pressure and teen culture collide with unprepared teens entering the hardest years of their lives.)

Some parents just don't think that bad things will ever happen to their children. They are confident that they are doing a good job of parenting, so their children will never go off the deep end. And most of these parents really are doing a great job.

But many underestimate the overwhelming effect this upcoming tidal wave of culture is going to have on their teen. They believe that all their good efforts and good work invested in their pre-teen will shield her from the barrage of influences that will present themselves the minute she steps on the public school campus. They haven't overestimated the goodness of their efforts; they've underestimated the power of the new teen culture. They're preparing for a few waves; I'm talking about a tsunami. As a result, the teen ends up feeling overwhelmed, underprepared, and lost.

Let me show you what I'm talking about.

I had recently returned home from my first year of college, and I left my parents' house to go to work one night. Someone had mentioned that a tornado watch was in effect for Tulsa County. I didn't think much of it. As it began to rain, gray skies turned to black, rain turned to hail, and easy breezes turned into deadly winds. I didn't expect it, I thought it would never happen, and I thought that tornados touch down in other cities, not mine. As a result, I didn't pay attention to the warning signs, I didn't prepare for the possibility, and I was frantic and at a loss about what to do when the tornado did come barreling down a hill into our neighborhood, destroying everything in its path—my home, my possessions, my dog, and our lives as we once knew them. Incidents like this are life-changing. Afterward, you see things other people don't see, you prepare in ways others don't think about, and you know what to do when the unthinkable happens. Many homeschool parents have experienced this same storm.

I know this because I've had hundreds of homeschool parents tell me the following.

- "I never knew how difficult it was going to be when my child entered public school."

- "I didn't know what my child didn't know until she faced the unknown."

- "My daughter changed overnight. She left for her first day of public school and came back the same day a different person."

- "Everyone told us, 'If you just teach these things, everything will be okay.'"

- "We should have spent more time allowing them to socialize with others."

- "My wife is worn out after homeschooling for six years, and now she's twice as busy trying to solve the problems that homeschooling caused."

Here's what teens, looking back at their homeschool experience, told me about their struggles upon entering the public arena.

- "My mother taught me what was important to her, not what was important to me."

- "I learned some good principles; I just didn't know how to apply any of them."

- "My parents always taught me that 'the world' was a bad place; I found that it was a good place and that I was just too judgmental."

- "I felt like the biggest dork when I went to high school. I didn't know how to talk, how to socialize, or how to act outside of what I knew in my family. So I tried everything to fit in. And that's when the trouble began."

Most parents who homeschool do so because they feel their local public schools will expose their children to danger, drugs, and negative peer pressure. Many choose to homeschool because of the flexibility of schedule, the active involvement and influence in their children's lives, and the opportunity to have a say in their education. These are positive concerns. The problems I see with homeschooled kids are not caused by their families' values but by their lack of exposure.

Many homeschool parents struggle with their teen because they spent more developing her into the teen they want her to become than in developing her into what she needs to be to survive the influences of the teen culture she is now being exposed to. Parents do well to remember to train their children for the world in which they will live, not the world they want them to live in.

When parents underestimate the power of the upcoming tidal wave of teen culture, and when a child is not prepared to head into these new waters, the young teen is in danger. Instead of receiving small waves of influence and exposure to alternative beliefs and social situations, homeschooled teens are often dropped into one tumultuous wave of new experience. Anyone standing on the beach watching this play out will surely see the impending disaster. Homeschooled teens who enter public or private school experience greater demands for social acceptance than do kids who grew up in that environment.

The inappropriate behavior I see in homeschooled teens is the same as the inappropriate behavior I see in thousands of other teens. But the motivation behind the behavior, the key to unlocking the door of reason and understanding, is often tied to going into public or private school for the first time. Here are the needs I have found.

The Need to Break Away

I met with a group of homeschooled teens and asked them to describe themselves in retrospect, looking back at their first week in public school. Here is a compilation of their comments:

- "I was easy to identify because I looked like a dweeb."
- "My jokes were old, my comments outdated, and my perspective stupid."
- "I thought I was a pretty neat guy until everybody started making comments."
- "We acted goofy."
- "I remember trying to start up a conversation about Christ and creationism at the lunch table in the cafeteria, and the kids laughed at me."
- "People looked at us like we were from another planet."
- "I was quiet."
- "I was scared to death."

- "The locker room scared me."
- "Some kid slammed my locker shut and mimicked me."
- "People were making jokes about me."
- "I felt lost. I felt like a fish out of water."
- "A few people were nice to me, but I just felt they did that because they felt sorry for me."
- "I never thought about what I was wearing until that day."
- "You could spot other homeschooled kids at school for the first time. One of the guys I met on a soccer team sat at another table and cried."
- "I felt socially awkward."

These comments came straight from formerly homeschooled kids. These descriptions may or may not be accurate, but it doesn't really matter. Kids respond to their feelings. Why? Because teens have a need to engage. Homeschool kids know they are different, and many strive within the first week of school to break away from the image others have of them. They'll mimic others' behavior to avoid their perceived homeschooled look. They might cuss for the first time. They might change their hairstyle. Young men may challenge others with brute strength when brains aren't accepted. They might smoke a cigarette for the first time, not because they love tobacco but because they love people and don't want to be different. Some teens will do anything with anyone to find acceptance. And the more awkward some feel, the more they'll try anything to fit in.

They'll come home asking for contacts instead of glasses. They'll make comments about needing their teeth straightened. The clothes that were once okay now aren't. Girls will want to wear makeup and don jewelry. Guys will want to change their look and attitude. They are trying to break the image that might come with the homeschool territory. If ridicule accompanies their transition into their new school setting, they will work hard to counter the comments and talk.

You may be thinking, *Now wait a minute, Mark! My child was homeschooled, and he or she is not a dork!* Count your blessings; you're probably not having troubles with your teen.

The Need to Fit In

A teen not only needs to break away from an image that is causing pain in his life, he also has a driving motivation to fit in. He may not want to be *of* the world, but he certainly wants to be *in* the world. Many times, the behaviors that help kids break out of the homeschool image can also help them fit in with peers. Wanting not to be different and wanting to fit in are driven by the same need for acceptance. Acceptance is a major drive for any teen.

How far will teens go to find acceptance by their peers? This strong desire and the opportunity to engage in more drastic and more dangerous inappropriate behaviors enable teens to quickly destroy an image and make a new connection with peers.

I've noticed two types of people in this world: plungers and dippers. I swam competitively for 13 years and spent a majority of those years attending early-morning swim workouts. Getting out of a warm bed and driving to a pool to jump into some cold water was not enjoyable. I learned that some people just dive right into the water to get the inevitable over with quickly. Others, like me, inch their way into the cold water. Toe first, knee second, then the legs, dip to the shoulders, and then submerge. It worked better that way for me. I got in the water, but I didn't have to take the plunge like my fellow swimmers.

Many homeschoolers are forced to take the plunge when they may be wired to do a little at a time. Protecting children for years, keeping them from social interaction with people their age, and then expecting them to adjust normally in a new pool is unrealistic and can overwhelm a teen. The second problem with the plunging technique is that some homeschooled teens haven't learned to make decisions, choose alternatives, and engage in compromise and negotiation in a social setting.

As early as first and second grade, children can learn how to make choices in situations that are not in line with the family's beliefs and principles. Situations like this can demonstrate whether the family's values are sticking. This also allows children to enter the socialization process early, while a parent still has some control, rather than plunging a child into an environment later where parents have very little control. I'm not advocating sending your child to public school early. I'm encouraging you to include opportunities for your child to inch his way into the socialization process, especially if he is not a plunger.

Learning to make good and wise choices at an early age will empower children to make good choices when they become teens. And believe me, you want them to make good choices when they are in their early adolescent years. I have been amazed at the number of teens who tell me that the first time they used drugs was when they were 12. Many have told me that their first sexual experience was at 13. Too many have said that they were drunk for the first time when they went to a seventh-grade party. This was the world they had to live in, but all of these teens said they weren't prepared for what they had to face.

The first time your daughter engages with someone who doesn't believe the way she does should be when the stakes involve a piece of gum, a place in the cafeteria line, or a toy she wants to play with. You don't want the stakes to be her sobriety or virginity.

Many homeschooled kids are not being rebellious when they act out or display inappropriate behavior; they are longing to connect and gain acceptance. Too many times, they are labeled as rebellious or troublemakers. Some will enjoy this new status even though it violates their beliefs and values. It's better than being an outcast with principles. Troublemakers achieve two things: They break away from an old image, and they win a place among peers. These homeschooled kids are settling for something of lesser value that now appears to be of greater value because of being thrust into teen culture for the first time and being expected to survive.

The Need to Catch Up

Many teens who have been socially out of the loop in their earlier years enter the teen years with a sense of contentment about their life. They may soon find out, when integrated into a new teen social environment, that they've missed out on a few things. Many feel a great need to catch up with others in their class. This is especially true of young people who have been homeschooled well into their high school years. When the identity of older teens revolves around what you have and what you've done, those who have been held back from such things might feel a need to engage in activities that will bring them up to speed. This could include any possession and any action.

I hear many kids say that once they got around other people and saw what they did and what they had, they wanted the same. I hear the same thing from older (12 and above) internationally adopted kids. Simply put, many teens don't know what they don't have until they see others who have it, and then the contentment they once felt turns into a longing for more.

The Need to Spread Their Wings

Some teens who have been restricted to a homeschool environment desire to spread their wings a little and see what they're made of. They want to know if their wings really work. They want to test flight. They want the outside validation of others who might choose to love them, rather than those (parents and siblings) who have to love them. They might want a stamp of approval from someone other than those who have always told them everything that was right about them. You can call it wanderlust, adventure, excitement, wanting to have fun, or just wanting to experience something new. They've been pent up, and they want to be turned loose. Some of that flying can get them into trouble.

People don't have to be around me long to know that I'm a believer in giving kids early doses of some good things and early doses of some bad things. Letting children experience limited and measurable doses of rejection, differing opinions, hurtful comments, and painful situations can help prepare them to enter the teen years. I believe that the earlier in life children learn to make choices and follow their conscience, the better they will make choices in the future. And I believe that iron does sharpen iron in the socialization process, even when you're six years old. This approach is not always easy, and it's not always fun, but it is, in my opinion, the most beneficial. I'm a dipper, not a plunger.

If your teen has plunged into the confusing adolescent culture and you're having some of the problems mentioned in this chapter due to some homeschooling issues, know that all is not lost. Everything you have built into your teen's life is still there. Maybe you can't see the growth of the seed, but it's there.

Let me give you some thoughts about what I've seen work with families that are experiencing what you are going through.

Acknowledge Your Mistakes

Somehow the mere fact that parents acknowledge where they have been wrong changes the tide on that beach that seems to be so tumultuous. You're looking for ways to calm the waters and get your teen back to shore. The best way to start is to admit anything you might have done wrong. Don't skip this paragraph because you feel you've done everything pretty well. No parent is perfect, and if your homeschooled teen is struggling now, something went wrong. You either didn't prepare your teen for the world he is to live in, or you have prepared him in the wrong way. For whatever reason, it's not working. When you tell your teen that you made a mistake by not preparing him properly, or you tell him that you were wrong in what you thought, what you believed, what you wanted, or what you desired for him, you release him from feeling as if something is wrong with him.

If your homeschooled teen is struggling, she may feel as if she is less than what she should be and worse than she actually is, which only fuels her drive to be something different. Usually, to be different, you have to act different. So to calm her waters, let her know that this problem is not a sign that anything is wrong with her. You can take this overwhelming burden from her and use it as an opportunity to come alongside her while you struggle together. Keep in mind that the issue has more to do with the teen culture than it does with wayward teens. Keep that perspective as you react and respond to your kids.

Set Some Strong Boundaries

Whenever the boat (your home) is tossing and turning on this sea of confusion and struggle, your kids need to know what they can hold on to and what will be secure. Make sure they understand the boundaries you set. Talk about this in a way that builds relationship. Do not be repelling and offensive.

Give In on Some Rules and Expectations

Ease the tension that your teen feels by releasing some of the pressure. This would be a good time to separate those expectations that matter from those that don't. I'm not saying you should lower your standards and drop your expectations. I am saying that this might be a good time to lighten up a little.

You can't hold on to everything all the time. As you get a little older, you'll let go of some of the things you hold so dearly now. Wouldn't now be a good time to give in a little? Could you benefit from letting go, rather than holding so tightly? Only you know what you hold tight. Only you can determine what you're willing to let go. If you had to give up three things, what would they be? Your stance on dress? Hair length? Dating? Curfew? Freedom? Old, outdated beliefs? Find three things and toss them out.

Give Him Something When He Least Expects It

Let your teen know that you're willing to make some changes to create an atmosphere where he can change. Many teens don't change because their environment doesn't allow it, and the only way to break down walls is to have a civil war. Take your family on a surprise trip. Purchase something that would let him know you are thinking of him.

Make Sure You Get Together to Talk

The counsel I give out the most but people follow the least is this: Go spend time once a week with your child and talk. This is the most productive activity any parent can do. Spend time and get through any shortcomings in your teen's life together, and I guarantee that the seeds you have sown in the life of your teen will come to fruition.

Be an Incher, Not a Plunger

Don't make all the changes for your adolescent at once. Fad diets for impatient people work in the short run but not over the long haul. Change a little bit at a time. This lets your teen know that she doesn't have to change all at once either.

Chapter 6

You Never Know Until You Ask

■ ■ ■ ■

The telephone call I received from one mom was pretty typical. My conversation with her son Will was shocking.

She started by telling me that her son had been a great kid and never caused any problems. But at the beginning of his junior year in high school, everything changed. After a few weeks of school, in the middle of the football season, he quit the team. (He was the quarterback and had led his team to the state playoffs the year before.) He became withdrawn, quit talking to his family, and distanced himself from all those around him in their small community. Mom stated that he woke up angry, was mad most of the day, and went to bed enraged. He dropped out of the church youth group that he had traveled on summer mission trips with and had recently walked away from a three-year relationship with his wonderful girlfriend. His grades dropped from A's and Bs to Cs and Ds. He was spending his hard-earned money, but she had no idea where it was going. He wasn't where he needed to be when he needed to be there, and he never shared where he had been once he came home.

Oddly, this mom didn't ask me a single question. She just shared her story. I finally asked this tearful mother how I could help her. She told me what she thought she should do, how her husband was frustrated and wanted to kick their son out of the home, and how his sisters were reacting to the slow loss of their brother. She didn't ask me a question, and she never answered mine.

I listened. I offered to help and then ended the conversation pretty sure that this dear lady probably had a son who was on drugs and she that didn't know how to ask for help for something she didn't even know she was facing.

She called a couple of days later to give me some more information. Again, she never asked me a question. I asked her what her son was telling her when she asked him questions. She replied that she hadn't asked him anything yet because they've been so busy just getting him to do better in school, grounding him when he disobeyed, and telling him that he couldn't be angry around his sisters. She told me that her husband was disappointed that his son had dropped out of football and didn't want to go hunting with him this year. The focus was most definitely on his behavior and what everyone was missing from this young man.

Nobody was asking him questions. I shared with her that it sounded as if they really didn't have a clue what was going on and were just trying to keep their heads above water by managing the behaviors and not diving into the real issues. She told me that not going hunting, the anger, treating his sisters meanly, dropping out of football, and making bad grades *were* the issues. I responded that those weren't the issues; they were the symptoms of bigger issues, and someone had to find out what was going on. I told her that I couldn't give any direction to her without sitting down with him. I invited her to come to Texas or to meet with me when I was to visit my parents in her city over the Thanksgiving holidays.

I met Will at a restaurant, where his mother introduced us and said she would return when I called. As we sat, I could tell that Will didn't want to be there, didn't want to be lectured by a stranger with a mustache and a big nose, and sure didn't like the idea of spending part of his Thanksgiving vacation with someone he didn't know. Our chit-chat about music, football, Oklahoma, and what he wanted to do after high school quickly faded into my barrage of questions just to find out if there were any sensitive areas that hurt to touch. Those areas were quick to rise to the surface. Shame filled his eyes, and he wouldn't make eye contact with me, a stranger. Tears ran down his face as he shared about each of the relationships he had with all his family members. Disappointment in himself came through all of his words—how he had let down the team, his parents, and his friends, and how he had violated all his own principles. After an hour of asking questions, I knew that the symptoms I saw had nothing to do with a drug or alcohol problem and that a secret needed to come out.

After I asked a few more questions and gave him a lot more assurances, he finally opened up. During the first week of school, he began a sexual relationship with one of his teachers, and it had been continuing for three months. Suddenly the veil was raised, and an understanding of his inappropriate behavior emerged as the burden of the secret was lifted from his shoulders. But an understanding of his behavior is not acceptance of it. I called his mother and asked her to bring his father, and we sat in the back of the restaurant as this family got angry, expressed emotion, hugged one another, and tearfully committed to "get through this." Will was markedly relieved now that the cat was out of the bag, and I remember the mother's first question to her son. She said, "Why didn't you tell us about all of this?" Will's answer was simple but poignant: "You never asked."

Will had many reasons for not going to his parents. Most kids know that any type of sexual relationship outside of marriage is wrong. This is why they're sneaky and unwilling to share their exploits and experiments. It's why they feel guilty. The added factor of being sexually abused, as this young man was, complicates the issue. When kids get lured into a relationship, they often continue in it out of fear that their participation will become known. They know they will then have to live through the consequences of their poor choices, wrong decisions, or inability to fend off the aggressiveness of another. Many teens shame themselves to the point of self-contempt and continue in the sexual relationship because of the temporary high of good feelings and emotional connection. Will couldn't go to his parents because of a small amount of his own willful participation in an act that was immoral, illegal, and deceptive, and he had much to lose if others knew of the fling. Sexual acts with a girl his age would be looked at far differently from the same acts with a teacher.

If he was found out, he would have been kicked off the football team and shamed by his youth group. He would have disappointed his dad. He would be confronted with his own violation of his principles and might even have to leave his small town because of the gossip. He would not be able to continue in his job if his employer felt he was deceitful. Teachers and school administrators would look at him differently. Parents would not want their teens to hang around him. Girls would ignore him. His friends wouldn't understand and would shun him from social events. How do I know this? Because this is exactly what happened.

So Will hid the relationship, and his anger became more and more evident as he dug deeper and deeper into the hole he could not climb out of. He wasn't really angry at his family. The anger he felt in other areas of his life spilled over onto his relationships within his family. This teacher quickly became his only friend by her determination and his default. Her manipulation of this young man for her own pleasure moved him to exclude all others. In reality, he was trying the best he could to survive in a world that was going dark quickly. That which a person will not talk about, he will act out. And Will's behavior spoke loudly.

Many in his town said he was old enough to know better. I would agree. But everyone knows better. Not everyone has an adult, who is supposed to be responsible and mature and trustworthy, tugging and enticing him in every way she knows how. Make no mistake, this is abuse by any definition. The teacher lured Will into something, and Will had to pay the price of his inability to say no.

Parents ask me all the time how I get teens to talk to me. I really thought my connection with teens would wane as I got older, but I've found that my relationship with teens and my ability to talk with them has really become much better. It's sure not because of looks or the way I dress. And teens are hardly impressed with a mustache or the fact that I can play the guitar, make them laugh, ride horses, or water-ski. My effectiveness seems to be wrapped up in two challenges: creating a safe environment for discussion, and asking questions and listening without passing judgment.

If parents asked more questions of teens in situations similar to Will's, the problems wouldn't have to escalate to the point that people are forced to demand answers. I have found that parents don't ask questions because they really don't believe that some situations and crises could really happen in the life of their child. Parents don't think their child will be abused, shot, beaten up, or raped. They don't think that babysitters, grandfathers, stepdads, teachers, or athletic trainers will sexually abuse their adolescent. They never consider that their adopted child might struggle, that their own child might be depressed, or that a brother might be abusing another brother. They don't think their child would commit suicide, get drunk, smoke dope, cheat on tests, shoplift, vandalize, or become sexually involved. They never really think that a youth minister might be inappropriate with their child.

Not believing these things can happen to their child, parents don't ask questions about the possibilities. As a result, parents inadvertently hand their child the shovel he needs to keep digging deeper into a dark and damaging hole of confusion and shame. Wise parents understand that any of the issues listed above can happen, and they prepare for the possible struggles their child might go through, thus giving him a hand up and out of any hole. Foolish parents never give it any thought. The most common comment I hear from the parents of hundreds of struggling teens is this: "I never knew this could happen to my child." Let me assure you from years and years of experience that anything can happen to anyone at any time.

The power of asking questions is amazing. When parents ask questions in a non-condemning way to a child who is struggling or displaying questionable behavior, they convey a sense of value and relationship that is unparalleled by any other act of kindness. The movement toward a teen by asking her about herself lets her know you have an interest in her, that you want to help her through her dilemmas, and that you're watching.

Engaging with your teen through the power of caring inquiry is crucial, but you must also learn to keep your mouth shut long enough to hear her answer. When it comes out, regardless of how bad or shocking it is, don't respond with words, anger, or disappointment. Just listen. Establishing a line of communication is far more important than getting your response across, especially if your first response cuts off service and keeps further dialogue from happening.

Sometimes, just by asking questions, you empower teens to apply the values you have taught them to their current situation. Your questions might encourage your teen to ask questions of you. And if she does start asking questions, she might be inviting you to a dark and shameful corner of her world. I know it works. I help teens get through their issues and problems by asking questions like these:

- What angers you the most about the world you live in?

- What are you not getting that you want so badly?

- What's been taken from you that you didn't want to give away?

- If you could get one thing back that you no longer have, what would it be?

- Is there something you always wanted but never got in life?

- Is there something that you know that I don't know that would change my perception of you?

- Who are you the angriest at right now?

- Do you ever have any dreams that turn into nightmares?

- What is your greatest fear right now?

- If you could change one thing about our family, what would it be?

These are all questions that engage your child and ask for something more than a yes or no answer. These get him thinking and invite him to open up without being judged. Your conversations with him send the message that you will not condemn him. Your condemnation is what your teen fears the most, so he'll shy away from the truth for the sake of saving his relationship with you.

Want to know why you sometimes don't know why your child is struggling? Maybe you haven't asked. You have not because you ask not. Don't believe you know everything that has happened to your child. Do your parents know everything that happened to you when you were growing up? No? So do you think you know everything that has happened to your teen? Sobering thought, I know. Try asking.

Chapter 7

More Lost Than Rebellious

■ ■ ■ ■

When I first met Lori and saw the loving way she engaged with all around her, I could hardly believe she was such a mess. On the outside, I watched a perfectly normal girl who was laughing, smiling, engaging in conversation, and even asking me questions about my life. She was interactive and affectionate. I remember telling her dad how sweet she appeared. He looked at me with his glasses on the end of his nose and said, "Just wait." We both chuckled. I replied that I hoped that one day we would stand at her wedding and look at this time in our rearview mirror, where issues usually appear smaller than they are right now. He responded, "I hope we get there."

On the inside, Lori was a wreck. She had been sexually abused until she was four years old. She was abandoned by her mother and abused by her other family members. She had suffered neglect and experienced the most horrendous toddler years anyone could imagine. She spent time in the foster care system until she was rescued by two of the finest people that walk the face of the earth. Life had not treated her well in her younger years, and now, as an adolescent, she was realizing, feeling and acting out all the hardships she experienced as a child. I learned in high school that every action has an equal and opposite reaction. And the grotesque actions this young lady had endured in her early years were now showing themselves ten years later in an equally damaging reaction.

So who was she? The Lori who was so engaging, approachable, cute, and relational? Or a product of abuse, neglect, hardship, and hurt?

A little of both, which she would have to learn to accept.

As I got to know Lori and spent more time with her, I noticed and experienced her bouts of anger—responses to something that had been pent-up for years. As her parents shared what had happened in her past, she began to relate her feeling to her damaged memories, and she began to understand the abuse and resulting damage that had happened in her life. She was hyperactive, which made it hard to keep her on task in dealing with her thinking and behavioral issues. She had a couple of learning disabilities that we had to accommodate. We all had to temper our frustration when she just wasn't picking it up as quickly as we all had hoped. She was impulsive, so emotions, mean words, and disrespect flowed when she was frustrated. Similarly, when she was in a good mood, accolades, hugs, and "warm fuzzies" followed. When she got mad, she was utterly disrespectful and hateful. When she didn't get what she wanted, she'd resort to fight or flight. When she was around guys, she didn't think. And she would act on any thought that came into her head, good or bad.

We quickly learned that this young lady had very few internal controls, so we needed to put her in a setting that had plenty of external controls. But putting more controls around Lori was like trying to cage a wild animal. Getting her in the cage was easy, but once she realized what we were doing, she resorted to her old ways, usually with more fight than flight. The ugly serpent of abuse raised its head at the craziest of times. Once, while we were at the lake waterskiing, she had a meltdown because she couldn't get up on the skis. She didn't think she looked good in front of others, and she felt that she was something less than we all knew she was. She started screaming at me, yelling that I was pushing her too hard and not driving the boat right, and cussing at the top of her lungs that we were trying to make her look bad. It was a major meltdown in the middle of the lake, and now was the time to help her through it.

Another staff person was in the boat with me, and I told her that I wanted her to drive off after I put on a life jacket and got in the water with Lori. As the boat drove off, Lori yelled and screamed at me as we were in the middle of a lake, hundreds of yards from the shore and a million miles away from the warm relationship I thought we shared. After 45 minutes of her yelling and screaming with nowhere to go, she calmed down. Out there in the middle of an East Texas lake, Lori realized that all the stuff that had happened to her was more than she could handle. She must have added a couple more gallons of water to the lake through her tears that afternoon. It was truly a turning point (although I did tell the staff never to listen to me again if I asked them to leave me in the middle of a huge lake). The time floating, yelling, and being hundreds of yards from shore was significant for Lori. At that point, she finally realized that she couldn't resort to her normal fight or flight patterns and had to face the issues that were staring her down.

She had been diagnosed by a psychiatrist with oppositional defiant disorder, attention deficit disorder, hyperactivity, uncontrollable impulsivity, depression, and more. She showed signs of all of these. The psychiatrist believed she was going to rebel against everything and everyone because of all the damage in her life and that it would eventually just go away. I thought differently. I didn't think that Lori was rebellious. I thought she was lost and couldn't find her way, much less know where she was going in life.

Which of us was right? Probably a little of both.

When she was upset, her adrenaline kicked in, and she quit reasoning, understanding, listening, or attempting to communicate anything other than that she wasn't getting her way. Her fuse was lit, the show was about to begin, and you better stand back 'cause she was gonna blow. All the hurt, anger, and disappointment she had felt in her life seemed to culminate in that one moment when she was taking control of her life and was not going to let anyone else control her. I was excited to see that she wanted control, but I wasn't so excited to have this Roman candle pointed at me. I was thrilled to see her fireworks display—a mixture of frustration for what had happened to her and a strong desire to take control of her life—but I didn't want to get too close for fear of getting burned.

Lori's behavior was explosive and sometimes hurt others, but it was also a healthy combination of realization and desire. She realized she had been hurt, and she desired something different. The problem was that the friction sometimes caused sparks that burned those around her. Most people only touch a hot stove once, and once anyone was burned by Lori's friction-filled actions, they didn't hang around long enough to get to the root of her issues. The subsequent departure of people from her life then affirmed in her mind what she always thought to be true: that she was not worthy of being loved or having anything good. She would again feel abandoned and alone.

The problem was in the way Lori was expressing her issues. Her actions had become habitual knee-jerk responses to any situation where she didn't get her way, she was not in control, or she felt that someone would abandon her. Nobody wanted to live with a case of dynamite. Our goal with Lori was to help her tone it down a little and not destroy the relationships around her with her temporary, sudden, and unpredictable outbursts. We helped her build some internal structures that would keep her focused in an environment with limited or no external structures.

The way I see it, if you have one drop of water in a glass, you're on your way to filling it. And Lori was no exception. My view was neither optimistic nor pessimistic. It was predicated on my belief that God had a plan for this girl (as He does for every teen). By recognizing the damage in her life. Lori made a first step toward repentance, which would eventually help her crawl out of the mess her life had become. My thought was that if she had one drop of water, she could eventually have two, then three, then four, and so on. With enough perseverance, she would eventually have a glass that was half full, which is better than half empty. And if she could get halfway there, surely she could keep persevering and get the other half filled. It was logical to me, and that's all that mattered because I was the one having to put up with the fireworks.

She eventually went home to Minneapolis, but the internal structures didn't last as long as we had hoped. The cycle began again. Lori spun out of control, stole her parents' car, got arrested, and spent a year in a juvenile facility. Upon becoming an adult at age 18 she hightailed it back to Texas, most likely because that was a safe place for her. Her dad called me to let me know she was coming to our neck of the woods. I saw Lori two days later.

She looked as healthy as the first day I met her. She was engaging, smiling, and full of conversation. She said, "I just have to do this on my own." We hugged and laughed about our lake incident, and she said she was off to find a job in our community of Longview, Texas. After a few months, she called and wanted me to come by the restaurant where she worked to meet her new boyfriend. I looked forward to that like going to the dentist. I didn't know what to expect, but upon meeting this new fellow, I was impressed, and Lori looked more relieved, calm, and settled than I had ever seen her.

A year later, I was standing outside of a small church in a podunk town outside of Longview with two sparklers in my hand as I watched Lori and her new husband run out of the church, get into their truck, and head off on their honeymoon. Time seemed to stand still. A many-year process was coming to an end, and I was thankful to see the hand of God molding this wonderful event. I panned the setting and for once saw people excited about Lori rather than always feeling disappointed in her. And this significant happening was taking place at such an insignificant place. Across the street from the church was a restaurant named Peckerwoods (can you believe that?). The sparklers were small, but it was appropriate that we had fireworks in our hands as we celebrated this wedding. They reminded us of all the fireworks we'd lived through with Lori. The church was small. The event was small, but what happened in that small church was something pretty big, and it was attended by Jesus Himself.

Lori's dad walked up to me in that parking lot and said, "This is what you were talking about seven years ago, isn't it?"

My response was simple as I gave him a hug. "I told you so." The man-hug with three pats on the back confirmed our mutual pleasure in what God had done with Lori.

Lori got married wearing a pair of white cowboy boots with pink stitching under her beautiful white wedding dress. She is now making good choices for her life. Life in the country keeps her calm. Her new husband keeps her focused. Her job working for a dentist keeps her active. The celebration at this wedding was far more than simply the joy of a new marriage. We all rejoiced because this young lady who had been lost was now found—not just found by a husband, but found by God and able to find her own relationship with Him. Maybe she finally found herself. She sure was looking and trying hard. Jeremiah 29:13 promises, "You will seek me and find me when you seek me with all your heart," and Luke 15:4 says, "Suppose one of you has a hundred sheep and loses one of them. Does he not leave the ninety-nine in the open country and go after the lost sheep until he finds it?" Luke 19:10 states, "For the Son of Man came to seek and to save what was lost."

Do you have a child who is lost? One who is not responding to what you are doing to help get her get to a good place? Many times, lost kids don't respond to their parents because they want to figure it out for themselves. I wish I could tell you that they will respond to your efforts, but that is not what I have found. Discipline that is put into play by parents often fails because the parents are trying to help a child get where he wants to be or to keep him from ending up at a place he doesn't want to be. Yet when a teen is lost, he doesn't know where he is, much less where he is going, so any attempt to get him somewhere or keep him from heading down a path of trouble is usually met with resistance. Parents can spend all the time they want telling their teen that the path he is on will take him somewhere he doesn't want to be, but it will usually have little effect.

But all is not lost. Just as Lori's parents rested in the Almighty's involvement in the life of their teen, you can rest assured that God is pursuing your child just as intensely as you are. And He won't stop until your wayward one is found. This doesn't mean you can just sit back and let God do all the work. He's going to use you in that process. As an old Russian proverb says, "Pray to God, but keep rowing to shore."

Here are four ideas to consider while your lost one is in the process of being found. These might help you keep your sanity and hope intact.

First, get into a small group of other parents going through something similar to what you're experiencing. There's nothing like having a crowd of people around you who are in the same boat trying to bail. Many times, people get involved in small groups just to talk. I would encourage you to get into a small group so you can also listen. When all you know to do isn't working, the counsel of others might spark some new ideas or directions with your teen. There is wisdom and comfort in the presence of many.

Second, gain an understanding of time, because you will probably see a lot of it pass before your lost one finds her way. It always takes a longer time to get to a destination when you're lost. To help in that passage of time, begin a journal of your thoughts, concerns, hurts, and struggles. Make it a prayer journal as well. I know that if I don't write something down, I forget it. Writing things down can remind you of God's presence in the midst of the struggle and encourage you later when you are able to look back and see how far you and your teen have come.

Third, offer good things when she is doing bad things. I know it doesn't feel right, but something about grace lays the groundwork for a teen to move back toward you when she finally comes to the realization that her life needs to change for the better. Teens who have been shown grace tend to move back toward people who have offered something and did not walk away from them. Many people ask, "Offer what?" Here are some ideas: Take her out to eat, fill her car with gas, bring home a new video game she likes. Remain mute for a day, offer to talk, suggest that you go do something together. This giving approach conveys the message that you can still love your child even though she is a mess, even though she is making mistakes and being hurtful. It lets her know that you can love her when she has it all together, and you can love her when she doesn't. Isn't this what we all desire?

Fourth, tighten the boundaries. Just because someone is lost, hurt, or damaged doesn't give him license to destroy you or your home, or constantly disrupt your family. One of my jobs at Heartlight is to repair fences in our pastures, to ensure that the boundaries are strong for our horses. They know where they can go and what is off-limits. When they break the fence, I fix it. When they push against the fences constantly and make them weak, I make them stronger. Boundaries, much like fences, protect. They define what's off-limits. Establishing and constantly keeping the boundaries in place ensures that your teen's wanderings don't cause you to lose your way. Even a child who is lost can learn to respect boundaries.

This is not an exhaustive list in dealing with lost teens. It is an additional list to many other things we've discussed in this book. Sometimes the best job parents can do is love their child and keep her alive long enough to either find herself or be found. If you hang in there long enough, what looks like an immovable wall will one day crumble. In the rubble, you'll discover some good things in your life and in the life of your teen.

Chapter 8

When a Parent's Good Intentions Go Bad

■ ■ ■ ■

hang out with people who cry a lot. Crisis and struggle have a unique way of bringing people to tears. Difficulty with a teen moves parents to emotions of all sorts, from intense anger to drop-to-your-knees surrender. There isn't a day that goes by that I'm not on the phone talking to parents whose hearts are full of sorrow, or who are just plain lost and drained of all emotion. My sympathy for parents and empathy for their current situation is, I suppose, one of the reasons that I am so moved to continue to fulfill God's call on my life to help families. But I've got to tell you, nothing moves me more than a dad who calls me in tears about his son. I get moved by many things—but this scenario, a dad crying on the phone, chokes me up the most by far.

I cried when Roger called me to talk about his son Adam, not because he described a son who was acting out and being disrespectful, but because everything Roger had tried wasn't working, and now he didn't know what to do or where to go for help. He told me he had done everything right in providing for his son, protecting him, and keeping him out of harm's way. He had done all the things his pastor told him to do. He said he and his wife had implemented concepts and principles they learned from parent conferences and couples' Bible studies. He had followed all the Sunday school lessons about parenting and listened to radio programs about family issues. He read books and searched the Web for articles on how to be a better dad. He said that he raised his kids God's way, was logical in his approach, and loved his son every way he knew how. He and his son used to have a great relationship, but now something wasn't right.

His question to me that signaled a deeper issue was, "How can something so well-intended turn out so wrong?" My eyes misted as I listened to this broken dad share his broken heart. I told him that I didn't know the answers to the questions he was asking but that I was willing to meet with Adam when I was to be in their city a couple of weeks later. His desperate comment to me was that he couldn't wait that long. Could he come to Texas tomorrow? I cleared my schedule to meet with Adam. This father's tears moved me not only to tears but also to invite him to come immediately.

Adam's behaviors at home sounded like most behaviors I hear about daily. Disrespect, dishonesty, cussing, surfing on the Internet where he should not go, and being rude to his little brother. Adam was disengaged, distant, angry, longing to get away from home, and struggling in school. Roger said that Adam's passiveness was turning into aggressiveness, and his once-silent demeanor was now turning into verbal destruction of family dinners every night. He shared how Adam would cuss occasionally and how his negative responses were getting stronger every time they enforced boundaries. Roger then shared that he and his wife were just doing the things they'd always done, but what once worked had now become unproductive.

Adam was a very cordial young man when we got together at a local restaurant. I thought that a public setting would calm his emotions and give me an opportunity to have "public image control" should something spin out. We spent a while just connecting, and then I started with my questions. I asked him to tell me about the difficulties at home, and he described them exactly as his dad had told me. I asked about all the behaviors his dad told me about, and he didn't deny even one. I asked him what he enjoyed doing, what he was allowed to do, how he related to others, what privileges he had as a 17-year-old, and what responsibilities he had to fulfill around the home.

Here's what he told me: Adam was allowed to watch only G-rated movies. He could listen only to Christian music, and even that was limited to what his dad liked. No rap, just because. He couldn't drive because his parents didn't think he was mature enough to handle the responsibilities of the road. TV was limited to a few channels—Disney, History, Discovery, and *Leave It to Beaver*–type programs. Adam was not allowed to date. He couldn't wear shirts with any insignia of any kind. He had to sing in the choir at church. He couldn't have a job because his parents knew he'd spend the money frivolously. They wouldn't let him go to school dances, even though he went to a private Christian school. He had to get his hair cut the way they wanted it. If he ever used the word *jeez*, he lost his allowance because *jeez* is a euphemism for *Jesus*. Adam's parents didn't allow video games and said no to any movies or TV programs that had an inkling of sex or violence. He had to be home for dinner every night and wasn't allowed to socialize with friends on school nights, even if there was a school-sponsored event or special event. He was allowed to go out during the week only to church for choir practice and various fellowship opportunities.

Adam shared that he loved his parents, but he also said, "They're killing me and won't let me grow up." He shared with me that he was beginning to be made fun of at school. He cried when he shared how people picked on him for not being able to do anything. He said that he was eliminated from his group of friends because he couldn't do what all the other kids (in a Christian school) could do. He choked up because he didn't know how to relate to girls, and it was embarrassing. He said that he would often kick himself for saying stupid things. He was insightful when he stated that he was moving away from his family, his friends were moving away from him, and he was stuck in the lonely middle. I teared up again as he shared his story. I thought to myself that I must either get more sleep, I must be going through a post-midlife crisis, or I was just plain hurting for this young man who was really a good kid struggling through pains of adolescence.

Something was so right in his parents' good intentions. However, something was also so right in Adam's intentions. Please note that I said his intentions, not his actions or behaviors. I understand inappropriate behaviors sometimes, but I never feel they are justified. So in this case, what did I do? I had a young man in front of me who I believed was right in his feelings, and I had a mom and a dad who were right in their feelings. Instead of having two rights continue to turn into this big wrong, I wanted to make this situation turn into something right for all of them, thus turning two rights into another right.

I wrestled with how to approach Roger and help him understand that his intentions were good, but the result was all wrong—not because of mistakes, but perhaps more because of miscalculations and these parents' lack of keeping up with the accelerating culture and social demands on Adam.

While I was trying to find an answer that would help steer all three members of this family in a good and healthy direction, I got a call from a young lady named Cindy. Well, she wasn't that young any longer, as she had served on our staff at Heartlight 20 years earlier. She and her husband wanted to go out to eat with my wife and me, so I agreed in a heartbeat. Halfway through the meal, she pulled out a stack of photographs and began to remind me of what I looked like when I was 33 years old (better-looking, much slimmer, and with hair just a little darker). As she reminisced about each picture and pointed out how I had deteriorated over time, I was consumed with another thought. I looked at the pictures and noticed that I was still wearing some of the same shirts I wore 20 years ago, thinking that they still worked for me now. Cindy assured me they didn't. As I left the restaurant, I just couldn't get it out of my head that I still had those shirts and still wore them. I had become so used to what I wore that I never took time to look at what was in my closet.

I knew that God had put Cindy back in my life for a reason, and the reason was to help Roger, Adam, and the rest of their dear family who, unbeknown to them, had the same problem I had with my shirts. I saw that Roger and his wife were perhaps carrying some old ideologies that were effective once but hardly applicable now.

I shared this story with Roger and his wife, letting them know that nothing was wrong with what they were doing in setting rules, standards, and expectations for their home. But just as my shirts were no longer effective because they were outdated, so were the rules they had placed around Adam. I shared with them that the response from Adam was really quite normal due to their outdated and unproductive constraints on their son. They were all well-intended but were not producing the anticipated results.

At first, they thought I was judging them. Their defense mechanisms flared, and they defended their strategy. I told them over and over that nothing was wrong. They just needed to update part of their strategy, throw out other parts, and formulate some new strategies to accommodate the changing times and the age of their son—just like my 20-year-old shirts needed to be weeded out of my closet.

Those shirts were kind of hard to let go of. They had been "friends" for most of my adult life. Honestly, I got a little mad at my wife's suggestion that we put them in a garage sale, and even a little nostalgic as I saw them hanging on a pole in our front yard and being handled by strangers. After all, they had served me well, made me look good, and always remained close.

It's hard to give up the familiar, but sometimes it's necessary if you want to make room for new shirts, new looks, and new styles—as well as when you want to meet the continually changing needs of your teen.

It's tough to hear that your plan isn't working and the path you're walking is no longer the right path. But let me assure you, once you get past the hurt and strain of understanding the need to change course with your teen, you'll feel a release of stress that you probably haven't felt in years, and you'll embrace change as an opportunity to deepen a relationship with your son or daughter. Changing will eventually feel much better than losing that teen.

Parents usually see their teen's inappropriate behavior and think something is wrong with their child. But the behavior is usually a natural response to provocation. Sadly, many parents don't see that they are the ones doing the provoking. As much as I hated saying it,

Roger and his wife were provoking Adam, and they interpreted his response to their provocation as rebellion. It was actually a response to loving parents who didn't know that they were setting him up to act out.

Who would have thought that Ephesians 6:4, "Fathers, do not exasperate your children; instead, bring them up in the training and instruction of the Lord," would pertain to the well-intended motives parents have for their children? The definition of *exasperate* includes a number of words that clearly describe the situation I see with so many teens today, words like *make furious, irritate, provoke, annoy, anger, inflame, infuriate, exacerbate, make worse, enrage,* and *aggravate.* I have always read Ephesians 6:4 thinking that the intent of the writer was to discourage dads from doing anything wrong in the rearing of their child, like cussing at a child, beating him, abusing him, yelling and screaming, acting selfish, sinning against the family, and other things that would cause a child to respond negatively. But children can also become exasperated over things that parents are trying to do right!

If your son or daughter is responding negatively to some of your well-intended actions, and those actions aren't working, it doesn't mean what you have been doing is wrong. Nor does it mean that you've been misled by those who encourage you to raise your child one way or logically love your child in another way. It's just that the teen culture has changed at such an alarming rate that some of those things that used to work and bring positive results may not be as effective today as they once were. You can't adjust the way your teen responds, so you might have to adjust what you have control of—your own rules and regulations—in order to initiate a different response from your child.

Roger and his wife had a hard time hearing this, but after a few hours of counsel, they dove into a deeper understanding of Adam's needs, as well as the need to change the way they had been operating. Here were my recommendations for them and their 17-year-old, college-bound young son: Let him go to some movies that are PG and PG-13. Open the door to other music while you can still influence him before he leaves home. Let him get his driver's license. Require him to get a job and pay for car insurance. Give him the opportunity to watch other TV channels at night. Allow him to date, as the influence of a young lady would help him greatly in his social skills. Let him make a choice about participating in choir.

Overall, I encouraged them to let the rope out a little more. Not to give Adam enough to hang himself, but enough for him to hold on tighter to the values and principles he's been taught. I told them that requiring more of Adam and asking more from him would empower him to take responsibility for his life and force him to develop maturity. He would acquire new social skills, calm his anger, and even give up some of his "old shirts."

Roger and his wife agreed with most of my recommendations, but they didn't accept all of them. And you know what? I didn't get rid of all the shirts in my closet either. I kept a few because some meant more to me than others. But this family moved to change, maintained their core principles, and let Adam know they wanted to be flexible and willing to compromise on some issues, and that sent a message of hope, relief, and relationship to a young man caught on the downside of some very good and well-intended parental limits and requirements.

Adam's parents were caught in a dilemma that many parents find themselves in today—having to make changes to accommodate the changes in today's teen's culture. Not to make those changes means that the way you teach principles to your teens may be causing more problems than your teen's participation in the very things you're trying to keep him from. That's a tough spot to be in. It's hard. Parents may feel as if they're violating their own standards and compromising their own beliefs. I'm not asking parents to do that. Rather, I am encouraging parents to look at the requirements for their teens and determine if there is any "wiggle room" within their structure to make some adjustments that would encourage a teen to stop his inappropriate and unacceptable behavior. The culture your teen is living in demands that you make some changes in the way you prepare him for his next major step in life.

I remember an old saying that came from a fellow I used to sail with in Branson, Missouri:

> A pessimist complains about the wind,
> An optimist waits for it to change,
> But a realist learns to adjust the sails.

What's in your closet?

Chapter 9

The Overprotected Teen

■ ■ ■ ■

wasn't expecting a call and didn't recognize the California number. When I answered I thought it might be our radio show producer. It wasn't. But the caller said his name was Phil, that Roger gave him my number, and that he was desperate. So I asked how I could help him. I remember Phil's exact words: "I'm struggling with my 17-year-old son, but I think my wife is the real problem. I'm not sure what to do. Can you help me?" I wasn't sure what to do either. I didn't know whether he wanted me to help him, his wife, or his son. He jokingly said that he needed the most help because if he had to live in the house another month, he was going to go crazy. We laughed a bit, and I asked him to tell me about his son.

He began to share how his son, Michael, had become increasingly disrespectful to his mom, yelling at her every time she began to speak at the dinner table, in the car, or in the kitchen. He said Michael leaves the house without asking, stays out past curfew, doesn't call to report in, won't listen to anything his mother asks him to do, and sometimes doesn't even answer her questions. Whenever Michael is disrespectful, Phil's wife expects Phil to discipline his son, which only exacerbates the situation and causes issues between Michael and him. He had started to skip school to be with friends, and Phil found some marijuana in the car. When confronted, Michael said, "You know why I smoke dope, Dad." Phil told me that at the moment Michael made that statement, he knew what Michael was talking about. And he confessed to me that if he had a mother like Michael's (his wife), he'd also have to find a way to relieve the strain of her incessant comments and hovering presence.

Phil told me that he loves his wife, that she's a wonderful lady, and that their marriage was made in heaven. He said nothing but good things about his wife. However, he did not say good things about Michael's mother—even though she is one and the same. She acted very differently with her husband than she did with her son. When I asked Phil to tell me about Michael's mother, it was easy to tell that he was frustrated, that he felt sorry for their only son, and that he thought that she was provoking the behavior they were seeing in Michael.

Phil said that his wife's role as a mother had always been a little "over the top," so involved in the life of their son that the marriage began to take a backseat to the parenting. Phil said she was so immersed in Michael when he came along that she became consumed with eliminating anything negative in his environment and providing everything he would ever need or want. That was fine when he was small, but as he grew older, she always wanted him to be clean, look cute, and have every toy ever made. Phil laughed as he told me that when Michael was seven years old, Phil would look out the window and see his son and friends all riding their bikes down the street, and Michael was the only one who still had training wheels on his bike because his mother didn't want him to get hurt. Michael had to wear "floaties" and a nose plug when swimming until he was ten because his mother was afraid he might go underwater and get ear infections.

Phil explained that their life as a couple began to revolve around their young son, and as Michael moved into his early adolescent years, Phil's wife got involved in everything. By the time Michael turned 13, he could do nothing—nothing right and nothing wrong—because his mother did everything for him. He didn't have to make decisions. He didn't have to remember anything. He didn't have to be responsible. He didn't have to earn his way onto a team because she would sign up to be the coach. If Michael was there, his mom was there. At

Michael's thirteenth birthday party, Phil and his wife allowed him to invite a bunch of his friends over for a coed swimming pool party. In the middle of the afternoon, Michael's mom came out to put sunscreen on his back so he wouldn't get burned. In ninth grade, when Michael's buddies had an all-nighter of movies and video games, his mother brought his toothbrush (with the toothpaste on it) to Michael so he could brush his teeth.

A verse came to mind when Phil told me about all of these incidents. It's a proverb that says, "Seldom set foot in your neighbor's house—too much of you, and he will hate you" (Proverbs 25:17). The Scripture right before that one is this: "If you find honey, eat just enough; too much of it, and you will vomit." Michael had a good thing in his mom, but as he got older he was beginning to hate the constancy of his mom's presence, and too much of a good thing wasn't leaving a good taste in his mouth.

Michael tried to talk to his mom and ask her to stop being so overinvolved. He asked her to stop preaching, lecturing, and teaching him all the time. He asked his dad to talk to her about her talking. Michael told me that he loved his mother when she was there, but he loved her more when she wasn't. When nothing normal worked at getting his mother to back off, he resorted to the abnormal. His justification for smoking marijuana was to "get rid of his mother's voice bouncing around in his head." He told me that he would cuss at her because that was the only way he could shock her into listening. He ignored her and was disrespectful in his silence as a way to keep his sanity. He stated that he was dishonest because it was the only way to get her to quit asking questions. He was disrespectful so she would leave him alone. He never thought about whether he was being disobedient because he never really listened to anything she said—she talked so much that he couldn't contain it all!

Moms commonly spoil and dote on their children. It's even quite normal for mothers to "baby" their sons through the early elementary school years. And as a son moves into his middle-school years, it can be quite appropriate to protect a child from some elements.

Normal development of a mother-son relationship would allow for that protection to lessen, however, by the time he turns 14 and moves into becoming a young man. My guess is that the overprotection in Michael's case did not reduce when he turned 14.

Michael knows, as every adolescent guy knows, that he must take more control of his life and develop a sense of responsibility and grow into maturity. Every male teen wants to become independent, make decisions for his life, and appear to be able to take care of his own. On the flip side, every 14-year-old guy I know also enjoys being pampered and catered to. Still, by the time Michael turned 16, the catering should have all but stopped as his need to be catered to and pampered properly declined. Michael's mother never let up.

When I met with Michael, I saw that he was well-balanced, he wanted good things for his life, and his behaviors, while inappropriate, were almost justified to fend off a dear-hearted lady who loved her son but was majorly overdoing it. When I met with her in Los Angeles, I was amazed at how wonderful this lady was and how much she loved her family. I was equally amazed that she didn't even realize what she was doing to her son. She thought that all her actions, involvement, and protection were loving provisions that she had never received from her parents. She was convinced that the more involved she was, the greater the level of protection, the better mother and parent she was being.

What was happening with Michael and his mother was interesting. Her efforts to be involved in his life weren't all wrong; they were just a little misplaced. She never realized until I sat with her that her actions were keeping her son from growing up, keeping him from being able to develop into the young man whom she really wanted him to be and who God designed him to be. Here's the kicker: Michael's behavior, for the most part, was intended to do both. Now, I'm not saying there is any justification for smoking marijuana. But I do think that his mother was "driving him to drink," so to speak, and when he couldn't find anything to drink, he resorted to what was available in his world. Teens always utilize what's available. Michael was no exception.

I'm sure that if I had not intervened in this family's struggle,

Michael's mother would have remained a wonderful but hovering helicopter parent, an apt description of parents who cannot let go of their kids when they go off to college. The sad part about being a helicopter parent is that when their children do leave home, the kids may have a hard time fending for themselves because they never had to assume healthy levels of responsibility.

I understand the Scripture that I've quoted in so many of the four hundred weddings I've performed. It says, "A man will leave his father and mother" (Genesis 2:24). It's inevitable. It's needed. It's healthy. And it's crucial to the future existence of a son who will one day be a husband, a father, and a grandfather. In every young man's heart of hearts, he knows this. Any attempt to thwart the normal development of maturity and independence in a young man's life will show itself in inappropriate behavior and acting out his frustration as he demonstrates his longing to become independent and self-sustaining. Michael was beginning the process of leaving so that one day he would spend more time cleaving to his future wife.

The fight that this family was experiencing was being caused by a well-meaning mother who didn't understand the effect of her good intentions. Michael's response, in one sense, was also well-intended, although inappropriately executed. The more time I spent helping each understand what was happening in their relationship and helping them see what they were doing to each other, the easier it was for them to break old habits of confrontation. New patterns of interacting were allowed to develop. In my humorous attempt to celebrate the way each had worked through their conflict, I sent them T-shirts picturing the cartoon character Yosemite Sam with both pistols drawn, and the caption "Back Off!" God, indeed, turned their sorrows into joy.

Helping Overprotective Moms Back Off

Moms don't intentionally overprotect their teens because they want to do the wrong thing. They do it out of a great sense of love. They were made to protect, and no one loves their sons more than moms. But as we've seen, the challenge is to love your teenage son in a healthy way that allows him to grow up and mature, to learn when to back off and let him take control of his life. Every decision that parents make for their son is one less decision he has to make for himself. Every responsibility that parents assume for their daughter is one more responsibility taken from her. Every day that parents keep their son dependent on them is one less day he has to become independent. Every dollar that parents give their daughter is one less dollar she has to earn. And every consequence taken away from a son is one less consequence that might teach him to quit acting in the way that caused that consequence.

Hopefully, you get my point about doing too much for your teens. Most parents' desire is to help their teen, but overprotection and over-involvement hinder them from raising a healthy, independent, responsible, and mature adult. If parents continue to do things their teens should be doing, those teens become dependent on others always doing things for them. That dependency quickly leads to an attitude of entitlement. Most parents in this country today know that we have a pretty entitled group of teens in our midst. But few of those parents recognize that teens are that way because of parents who overprotect, usurp responsibility, and give their kids everything. Most parents want a healthy, independent, responsible and mature teen, but we have not because we ask not. What we are asking of our teens is minimal. As they reach later adolescence, they become angry at parents who have overprotected and held them back, frustrated that they want to achieve but know only how to take. This results in a lack of ability to function in the world in which they will soon be required to live.

Here are some communication pointers to help you be a part of your teen's maturity in a positive way as he moves through adolescence into adulthood. Remember, moms have a way of not letting go of their sons quickly enough, and dads have a way of expecting mature thinking and choices from their teens when they haven't prepared them to be mature. Backing off, letting go, and giving opportunity for a different level of communication is essential in that development of mature thinking.

Quit Talking So Much and Let Them Talk More

When parents ask me how to better communicate with their teens, I usually start with his: Quit talking. I encourage parents to go home from our seminars and retreats and spend the rest of the day around family members saying nothing. Most are amazed at the results. Parents who accept the Shut-Up Challenge all express surprise at how many questions their teen asked them—for the first time in a long time. They share how their quietness forced someone else to talk. Of course, I tell parents that even a fool appears wise when he keeps his mouth shut. Because of the appearance of wisdom, teens then pursue parents to seek some of that wisdom, rather than parents always having to shove wisdom down their teen's throat.

Mom, you're usually the guilty party. Sometimes you just plain talk too much and don't give your teen an opportunity to talk. Many moms have a tendency to tell teens what they're going to tell them, then tell them again, then tell them what they just told them. It's a natural desire for moms to make sure they get their point across. But this method of repeating information has a way of pushing teens away and shutting them down. Teens comment to me all the time how they wish their mother would just be quiet and listen. When a mother corrects everything, gives an answer to questions that haven't even been asked, and constantly shares her opinion, teens shut down verbally and then find others who will listen to them.

The habit of always reminding, constantly teaching, and forever correcting is a training exercise that can be effective with preteens. When used with teens, however, the same tool becomes counter-productive. Moms, you don't have to have the answer to everything. Every question you answer is one less answer your teen has to figure out. Give her a turn. You've had your 13 years to pour your heart out verbally; now it's time for her to take all the good lessons you've taught and put them into practice. I would encourage all moms to spend one day not saying anything and to note what happens. You might find that your value in your teen's eyes rises substantially, and you might give your teen the responsibility to step up to the plate

and initiate conversation, enter into dialogue, and have a meaning-
ful discussion.

Double the Amount of Time That You Listen

Not talking is one action. Listening is another action. Just because
you're not talking doesn't mean you're listening. God gave us two ears
and one mouth because He wanted us to listen twice as much as we
talk (okay, not really, but it gets the point across). You may hear what
your teen is saying, but are you really listening without trying to correct him or get him to answer the correct way? When teens share
information and opinions, they're usually taking verbal inventory,
sorting things out, and thinking out loud. Parents hear this sometimes
illogical ranting and take offense because it doesn't make sense. The
resulting parental comments lead to arguments, and the parent misses
the heart behind the child's ramblings.

If a teen shares what is on her heart, and that is missed by a parent
more concerned about the delivery of the message than the content of
the communication, that teen will eventually quit sharing. All teens
want to do is talk and have someone listen to them. If your teen is in
the shutdown mode, there is a reason. And the reason may be that
you don't listen to what's being said anyway. Want to know if you're
a parent who doesn't listen well? Ask your teen.

Dad, if moms are usually guilty of talking too much, you're usually guilty of not listening. You're made that way as well. You don't get
distracted from your focus very easily. It's a great asset to have in the
business world, but it's your greatest liability at home. So many times
dads are only thinking one way, and anything different fails to get
through their filter. Dads, it's time to change the filters. You don't have
to work so hard to listen to your children when they're little because
they think you're Superman and can do no wrong. But when they enter
the teen years, they know better. You have to work at it now.

I would encourage you to sit down with your teen in a setting that
is conducive to asking questions and seeking information. When you
do this, try to focus on the heart of what is being said, not the logic.

If you are willing to just listen, you might touch the heart of your teen and convey a sense of value. Don't worry about what your answer is going to be; focus on the way your teen will hear your wordless message by the way you listen as she shares her heart.

Don't Share Your Opinion Unless Asked

This is a tough one. We all like to share our opinions, don't we? The mere act makes us feel as if we count. I'm reminded of Proverbs 18:2: "A fool finds no pleasure in understanding but delights in airing his own opinions." In a world where everyone shares his opinion in every newscast, newspaper, magazine, and reality TV show, it's hard to refrain from imparting wisdom to your teen. But I don't share my opinion with teens until they ask. If they want to hear something from me, they'll ask. If they want to know my opinion, they'll ask. When they do, I'll accept the challenge as an invitation to ask them questions too and to bring them to a point of searching more. Understand this clearly: *If they want your opinion, they'll ask.* They'll ask because they believe you are wise—why, you've taught them everything they know! But you've got to give them a chance to do so.

Quit Answering All the Questions

When they do ask you questions, don't answer them right away. The quicker you are to answer, the sooner they are to quit searching and reasoning for themselves. We spoil our kids rotten by giving them all the answers and not allowing them to search and enjoy the journey. We ruin the opportunity for discovery. We keep inquisitiveness and curiosity from teens' lives by too quickly jumping to give them the answers. Our answers have an amazing way of feeding their entitlement, their demands, and their need for instant gratification. Take the opportunity to stretch their minds, teach them a lesson, and get them to ponder and wonder about something more than just the answer they seek.

A parent's overprotection can keep a teen from trusting the protection of God Himself. And teens need to sense His protection as they seek Him, get to know Him, and trust Him to meet other needs in their lives. If we trusted God when our kids were preteens, we must also trust Him with our teens. When we get in the way of what God might want to do in the lives of our teens, then perhaps the fight we see from our teens—no matter how inappropriately displayed—could be an attempt to connect with the One who made them and wants them to grow into more dependency on Him and less dependency on us. It's tough to let go, and at times, it's tough to trust God with our teens. But letting God increase in the life of our teens by decreasing our control is a wonderful way of helping our teens grow and mature.

Chapter 10

Top Ten Reasons Why Christian Kids Rebel

■ ■ ■ ■

Many Christian teens rebel, just like teens from any other group. And Christian kids have some common issues to deal with that others don't. Others have unique issues as well, so no one is saying that one group of rebels is any better or worse off than the other. But some issues are unique to Christian teens simply because they have been raised in Christian homes. This chapter reveals the reasons that teens raised in Christian families listed as causes of their rebellious behavior. I discovered these reasons when I asked hundreds of teens, "What caused you to rebel against your parents?"

Every parent I've met would agree that the world is working against just about everything parents are working for in the life of their child. I'm *not* saying the world is a terrible place! I just believe it's a challenging environment for teens and for parents who are trying to train up a godly child. The task certainly isn't hopeless, but it calls for a new approach to the way we train our teens.

"Train a child in the way he should go, and when he is old he will not turn from it" (Proverbs 22:6). This verse was not intended to be an indictment of parents or a stick that measures the effectiveness of their training skills if their child temporarily departs from Christian values. It was given as an encouragement for parents to be intentional about teaching and building godly principles and precepts into their kids' lives.

You're probably reading this book because you're having more difficulties with your teen than you are successes. I would encourage you not to quit training, but to understand the challenges your child is facing in today's culture. That enlightenment may change some of the ways you relate to and transfer information to your teen. This doesn't mean that your big picture is wrong. It's just that more effective ways to accomplish the goal may be available.

I've spent much of this book sharing my perspective about the reasoning behind a teen's behavior, suggesting that a lot of the negative and inappropriate behavior seen in today's teens is a response to situations, actions, or choices in their lives. I believe that most of the behavior that is considered rebellious is really just a response or reaction to what's happening in a teen's life. Of course, some teens are deliberate, calculated, and determined to cause pain, problems, hardship, and turmoil in their parents' lives. But I believe most teens would like to have good relationships, put away their bad habits, get rid of their anger, and succeed—they just don't know how else to respond to what's being heaped on them at every turn.

Out of all the answers I've received from Christian teens about why they act rebelliously, ten stand out through the years. I'll reveal those in this chapter, share my perspective on each, and then offer some questions you can use to determine whether you might have given your teen a reason to rebel.

1. "My parents expect way too much of me."

Matt appreciated his parents' desire to want good things for him, but he felt they constantly ignored his pleas for some relief from the constant demand for more. Their overly high expectations moved him to feelings of disappointment and discouragement. He felt he could never reach the level his parents hoped for him, and those feelings moved him deeper into despair and eventually despondency. In an effort to stop the flow of constant expectations, Matt felt his only remedy was to shut down.

He tried to talk to his parents and ask why they expected perfection from him, but their answer seemed inadequate and made him feel his need was ignored. "Because I said so," they said, and that did not sit well with him. Matt and his parents found no better ways of communication, and their former relationship of respect and understanding from his younger years transitioned into a militaristic style of relating that had already destroyed a previous generation of relationships in this family. Now it was happening again.

- Are your expectations for your child too high?

- Is your teen confident he can satisfy your expectations?

- Are academics, social positioning, and appearance your teen's most important issues for right now?

- What would it mean for your child not to perform at the high levels you desire?

- Is loving an A student easier for you than loving a C student?

- If you asked your teen if your expectations are too high, what would he say?

2. *"I thought God was supposed to make life perfect, and it certainly wasn't, so I took my anger out on my mom."*

Brittany was raised in the church and enjoyed participating in every youth event and mission trip. Her mom told me Brittany was the most fun-loving junior high kid she knew. Brittany spoke before the church several times, went to Bible studies, and worked with the little kids in the nursery. She memorized Bible verses that stated how abundant life would be with Jesus, how God would never leave her or forsake her, how God had a plan for her life, and how God would protect her.

But Brittany's sophomore year was a tough year. Her dad died. A boy took advantage of her on a bus while going on a youth mission trip. Some other girls took pictures of her in the gym class shower and distributed them to all her guy friends. Life turns on a dime, doesn't it? Brittany got mad. She became angry and sinful, and her life began to fall apart as she felt loss, rejection, and betrayal. The truth now felt false. Life wasn't perfect, she didn't feel protected, nothing about her life was abundant, there was no plan in sight, and she felt forsaken. Her mom became the lightning rod and began to endure the powerful blasts from a daughter whose life had become a raging storm.

Life wasn't the perfect picture Brittany was told it was going to be. People didn't treat her like the princess her dad had told her she was. She felt that God had abandoned her and that she was lost and alone on some forgotten highway. Was it rebellion? Her mother said it was, but I thought it was more vengeance—not for what God had done, but for what He hadn't done.

- Have you taught your child that a relationship with Christ guarantees a wonderful life?

- Have you fueled you child's belief that if you just do certain things, everything will turn out all right?

- Have you ever shared with your son or daughter God's promises to be there during the hard times rather than promises to prevent the hard times?

- Have you taught a gospel of prosperity, only to find out that your daughter has experienced a world of poverty?

3. "My parents held me to high standards so they'd look good, not because it was good for me."

Blake complained and complained to his parents that they never understood the effect of the high standards they placed on him. He tried to explain to them that he felt they just wanted certain things from him because they didn't know what else to require. Blake's parents made comments to him like these:

- "You're not like Billy, so quit acting like him."
- "What would other parents think?"
- "You wouldn't say that in front of your youth minister, would you?"
- "God desires more for you."
- "You're a Smith, so act like one."

The parents' intent was good, but the delivery was bad. Blake felt as if he had to perform at a high level so he wouldn't be an embarrassment to his parents. His pleas for understanding went unnoticed. So he finally decided to get their attention and prove that he was more important than the neighbors' and friends' perception. In this case, his response to his parent's comments looked like rebellion. He chose behaviors that weren't necessarily selfish but that hurt his parents. Blake intentionally got into trouble at school—a calculated behavior to cause his parents pain. He engaged in activities that would draw attention to his rebellion. Tattoos, piercings, long hair, the way he dressed, his attitude in front of other parents, and his foul language were all a part of a scheme to embarrass his parents.

Many parents want their child to do well for the sake of being a good reflection on their parenting abilities. For some reason, many parents would rather look good in front of others than see the true heart of their child, who is actually longing for a deeper connection.

- Have you missed your teen's pleas for help?
- What is the motivation behind your desire for your teen to do well in social, academic, or other arenas?
- Have you asked your teen if she understands why you want good things for her?
- Have you let her know that you understand how hard it is to maintain a high calling and standard in their culture?

4. "My rebellion was to get my mom to quit being so overprotective in every part of my life, and to stop my dad from being so involved in everything."

Our generation of parents has been wonderfully involved in the lives of our kids, building values and character and developing relationships in their lives that were somewhat absent in ours. But too much of a good thing has a way of turning bad. Many parents have become overly involved, overprotective, and too controlling of their teen's life, thus forcing the teen to resort to behaviors that push away the parents.

Many times I've met with mothers and fathers who have become so dependent on their teen's relationship and presence that it is hard for the teen to move toward independence. Mothers sometimes find in their son what they don't find in their husband, and fathers find in their daughter what they don't find in their wife. Though rooted in love, these types of dependent relationships do not allow the natural quest for healthy independence to take place. When this happens, many teens initiate the separation process, and they may go to great lengths to rebel against their current unhealthy relationship to attain healthiness in their own life. This is one of those rebellious styles that *is* a healthy rebellion. The question before parents is whether or not they are causing it. Remember, true rebellion is intentional and aimed at causing pain or hardship in one's life. Rebellious behavior in the search for independence pushes a dependent parent away because the teen is unable to pull away on his own.

Max was one of those teens who unsuccessfully tried to get his parents to back off, and he eventually resorted to behaviors that destroyed his relationship with his mom and dad. He shared with me the reasons why he did what he felt he had to do, but he didn't admit his faults and apologize. He was not sorry for his disrespect, meanness, displays of anger, and ignoring of his parents. He believed that the loss of the relationship was collateral damage in his pursuit of freedom and healthy independence.

- Are you too involved in the life of your teen?

- Is your over-involvement an attempt to meet your own needs or to meet the needs of your teen?

- Do you find your teen telling you things like, "Quit!" "Leave me alone," "Mom, stop!" "Dad, I'm okay," "Would you guys just back off?" "I'm not a little kid; quit treating me like one," "Why do you have to know everything?" and "I feel like you're stalking me?"

- Have you asked your teen lately why she feels the need to hang out in places where you are not?

5. "My dad would always say, 'It doesn't matter what you think, God told me...' I wanted to punch him every time he said that."

Lauren told me that it was hard to live with God. No matter what she did, said, or thought, her dad would counter her comments with verbal blasts of Scripture and demands for submission. Her dad thought he was being helpful; Lauren didn't. In discussion around the dinner table, when Lauren asked spiritual questions, her dad told her what God's opinion on the matter was and demanded that she think the same. He wasn't comfortable with someone reasoning differently than he did.

Lauren's rebellion against her dad began when she had an epiphany that perhaps God was talking to her as well. After all, she had been taught that she had a personal relationship with Him through Christ and that she didn't need an intermediary to connect with the Father. It blew up one night when she stated to her dad, "If God is comfortable with my questions about who He is, why can't you be?" That statement didn't go over well. Dad interpreted her question as a challenge to his God-given authority in the home, and he told her she could leave if that's the way she thought.

She did. She left because her father couldn't give her the freedom to wrestle through her own relationship with God. This dad seemed to think that any questioning was a threat to his authority or a judgment against him and against God. Lauren and her dad were like two mules kicking each other; they were each stubborn enough not to give in.

- Is it hard for you to hear your teens question what they believe? Why?

- Do you interpret their unbelief or questioning of their beliefs as your fault—that you didn't train them right?

- Do you believe that you are more concerned about your child's welfare than the Great Shepherd is?

- Is it hard for you to allow your teen to "wander around" a little bit and check out what she's been taught? Why?

- If you're stubborn, are you holding on to some outdated beliefs about parenting teens?

6. *"My parents made a big deal out of everything I did wrong, and they never paid attention to the positives in my life."*

Madison lied to her parents all the time. She did it because she didn't want to be nagged to death by her mother, who picked up on everything Madison did wrong or didn't do quite right. For Madison, to lie and take her chances on the consequences was easier than to be honest and have to put up with the constant belittling from her mother. She stated that the only time she and her mother got along was when Madison lied to her and they were able to sit down and carry on a false conversation.

Mom couldn't see the A's on her report card because of the presence of the one B. Mom never asked about good things that were happening in Madison's life because she couldn't get her attention off the normal mistakes that any teen would make. She couldn't see how clean the whole house was because of the one smudge that was still on the window.

The problem escalated when Madison got into big trouble and didn't have anywhere to turn. She relied on immature friends and foolishness to resolve issues that were much too big for her to overcome on her own. She needed her mother when things fell apart, but her mom wasn't there because she had driven Madison away with her constant nitpicking and nagging. Ever remember reading about Samson and Delilah? Samson could not withstand Delilah's nagging: "With such nagging she prodded him day after day until he was tired to death" (Judges 16:16). Madison couldn't withstand her mom's nagging. As a result, the mother-daughter relationship died. It was a connection Madison desperately needed but lost because of a mother who spent more time highlighting the negative than she did affirming the positive.

Madison's response was silent. She eventually quit lying because she quit talking. She quietly went off to school after graduation and quietly lived her life in a new world that saw some good in her and accepted her when she wasn't perfect. Her lying habit went silent too as she surrounded herself with people who accepted her as she was.

At Madison's wedding, her mother got up to speak and share about her relationship with her daughter. With a smile on her face, Madison's mom shared how proud she was of her daughter even though she didn't include her in any of the plans for the wedding. She commented on how she was so happy that she was marrying such a wonderful fellow who would now have to put up with all of Madison's "stuff." Everyone in the room was silent...including Madison.

- Do you major on the minors and comment on flaws in your teen's life? Why?

- Would your relationship with your teen improve if you spoke half as much as you do?

- Is nagging your attempt to make things better or to tear things apart?

- Is it hard for you to have a child who doesn't have it all together and never will this side of heaven? Why?

- Does a flaw in your child reflect a flaw in you or your parenting abilities?

- How might you have caused your child to feel the need to lie to you?

- Could your teen's inappropriate behavior of lying be an attempt to keep your relationship intact?

7. *"If my mother's mouth was open, she was correcting me. My rebellion was to try to get her to shut her trap."*

Pointing out flaws and making corrections are two different things. In the previous example, Madison felt her mom paid too much attention to what she did wrong and no attention to what she did right. Casey's mother was different. She not only pointed out anything wrong or inconsistent but also went on to elaborate on the correct alternative. She elevated herself by being a know-it-all and having all the answers. Casey felt that his mom was always correcting him, and he knew that it wasn't for his benefit—it was for her benefit.

Casey's mom was determined to be in on every conversation around her and to correct any misinformation, which made her attempts to engage backfire. Both her husband and Casey would drop hints and even try to talk to her about how she came across, but she just couldn't be corrected. Her husband went "dark," and her son went "verbal." His tirades escalated to four-letter words that would make a sailor blush as he tried to shock his mother enough to get her to quit talking.

Mom told me that Casey had an anger problem. Casey agreed and said that he would continue to do what he had to do to keep his mother from driving him nuts. He told me he wasn't going to allow his mother to do to him what she had done to his dad. Oddly Casey's mother ignored any suggestion that she was contributing to his anger and that she could improve their relationship by changing herself. So we spent our time with Casey, helping him learn new coping skills to deal with a habit his mom wouldn't correct.

- How often do you say to your teen, "I don't know"? Is that difficult? Why?

- How often do you resist the temptation to correct a wrongdoing?

- Do you need to have an answer for every situation?

- Is it hard for you to remain silent so your teen can figure something it out?

- Does your spouse feel that you are quick to correct?

8. *"I had never been exposed to anything, so when I got to see what all the talk was about, I went nuts."*

I was raised in New Orleans, and every year on Fat Tuesday we packed out my dad's office in downtown to attend the Mardi Gras celebration. Most people wore costumes to the festival. We were used to Mardi Gras, what it was about, what went on, and what the celebrations were like, so we always wondered why people came from all over the country to participate. Did they know something we didn't know? Was that why they acted and carried on the way they did?

Oddly, those from out of town were usually the crazy ones. Drunk, obnoxious, and loud, the visitors who trekked to New Orleans for this yearly tradition were usually the out-of-control partyers. My brother, our friends, and I just walked around, waited for the parades to begin, and caught some trinkets and trash in hopes of snagging the coveted King of Rex doubloon. We could tell the natives from the out-of-towners.

What I saw back in the '60s never enticed me to want to drink, carouse, and make a fool of myself. Seeing others' actions didn't pull me in and make me want to do those things. I remember thinking, even when I was 12 years old, how stupidly some people acted. I wasn't enticed—I was repulsed by their behavior, and as a result, it strengthened my commitment in what I knew was the right way to behave.

Here's my point: For some reason, when teens are never exposed to the world and are intentionally shielded from it, they sometimes develop a grandiose perception of bad behavior. They hear about it and somehow glorify and magnify it into something that it's not. Their curiosity can get the best of them when they finally have the chance to experiment. They become like the visitors to New Orleans who make Mardi Gras out to be more than it actually is and behave in ways that others do not.

Katie's parents homeschooled her, were strict with her social interactions, didn't allow her to befriend other kids who weren't in their circle, and didn't allow any exposure to anything contrary to their beliefs. As a result, Katie didn't know how to act or respond when she entered the real world...and she went wild. I mean *wild*. If you can think it, she did it. If it burned, she smoked it. If you could swallow it, she drank it. And if it felt good, she did it (and sometimes did it again). Katie said she intended to make up for lost time and take advantage of what she had always heard about. Just like the visitors to New Orleans, Katie had magnified stories about the life that evidently, in her parents' eyes, God was not able to handle.

Katie believed that the world outside her parents' Christian bubble was bigger and brighter than it actually was. Consequently, she came to believe that God was evidently smaller than she had been taught. She also understood her parents to say that God didn't like the world and that she should avoid it.

That's not in the Bible I have. Mine says God loves the world, and it says He wants us to be in it and not of it. He also desires for us to be lights among the darkness. So if the world Katie dreamed about was bigger than the real world, and the God that she was taught about was a lot smaller than the real God (based on her parents' fear that He can't handle what's out there), then really it's no surprise that Katie became the out-of-towner partying at her own Mardi Gras.

- Are you afraid of the world?

- Is your role as a parent motivated by fear or by faith?

- Do you focus on protecting your teen or preparing her for new freedom and responsibility?

- Do you believe that God is as concerned about your teen and as involved in her life as you are?

9. "My dad is a pastor, and he is the most judgmental person I know. My rebellion was my way of paying him back for all his cutting me down."

Dan would be consumed with anger because his dad's sermons seemed to judge everyone but himself. Dan told me many times that he felt his dad's Sunday preaching was aimed directly at Dan. He said his dad turned whatever happened the previous week in their family into a sermon for all to learn from, presenting himself as being right and everyone else wrong. Dan said, "Dad forgot to tell the whole story," and his father conveniently left out the parts where he was wrong. Dan felt his father instigated many of the problems, handled them badly, and adjusted the real outcome in his sermon so that the church audience heard a story that was always a little different from what had actually occurred at home.

When Dan said something to his dad about this, he was met with silence. His dad wouldn't even enter the conversation about how distorted the sermons were, and he acted as if everything was okay after the Sunday service. Dan was hurt, he was damaged, and his anger turned to rage. He rebelled in order to embarrass his parents. It worked. Dan said, "I was out to get him for all the times that he set out to get me. The difference was that I wasn't afraid to admit it. He was."

No questions needed here, just a mirror. Is that a reflection of you?

10. "My parents were just so old-fashioned that my rebellion was a way to help them keep from being so clueless."

When I asked Cindy why she rebelled, her first response was, "That's easy. My parents were like Amish on steroids." Our whole grouped roared with laughter as we heard her description of what her home setting was like. Yet the antics that Cindy pulled to spite their strict rules and the truth about her home life were not laughing matters.

Cindy's parents believed that the old ways of parenting and the old ways of raising teens were good ways. They believed in the good ol' days. Their intentions were good, and their motives for wanting to protect their daughter were good. They were good people. But their old-fashioned ways clashed hard with the culture—and Cindy was caught in the middle.

Her parents wouldn't let her go out during the week. They wanted to have every family meal around the dinner table. They required Cindy to wear dresses to school. They allowed only Southern gospel music in the house. She was never to question authority, anything she read, or any directive her parents gave her. She was still spanked at age 15, and her mom believed that the dishes had to be hand-washed every night. Old hair styles, no makeup, and the family had to sit together at church. The combination of all of these requirements was too heavy for Cindy to carry. So when she dropped all the rules, her dad disciplined her—you guessed it, the old-fashioned way. His style of discipline didn't correct Cindy; it humiliated and infuriated her, and everything spun out of control. After Cindy had lived at Heartlight a while, she commented that she had more freedom here than she did at home.

- Are you holding on to some outdated beliefs for your family that are preventing you from offering your child what she needs to live in her culture?

- Are your requirements for your teen drawing her closer to you and God or pushing her away?

- Is your need to parent winning out over the needs of your teen?

- Do you hold on to old habits that are not working? Why? What other methods could you use?

- Might your teen's rebellion really be a cry to have you meet more of her needs at a higher level than your beliefs currently allow?

11. "No matter what I did, my parents always added something to it. There was always more, and whatever I did was never enough."

I know I said we'd look at ten reasons, but some parents always add just one more thing. There's always something else, another item, one more rule, one more requirement.

Taylor lived that life. He always felt he was just a little bit short of accomplishing anything. He felt as if he could never finish. He would mow the yard at home, run the Weedeater around the house, and blow off the driveway, and still his mother would find "just one more thing" for him to do. He would wash the car and detail it, but when his dad would come out to look, there was always something else that needed to be completed. Taylor told me that he brought home straight A's from school and was so proud, and his dad commented, "Maybe you ought to take some advanced classes."

Well, maybe Taylor could do that, and maybe he should do that. But the timing of Taylor's parents' comments always made Taylor feel as if he wasn't good enough, and he never would be. So he quit. It wasn't that expectations were too high, but there was always another hoop to jump through or a reminder that Taylor could go a little higher.

- Does your teen know he can accomplish what you ask him to do?

- Do you look for opportunities to praise your teen's efforts?

- How often are you content with what your teen does?

- Does your teen truly believe you're proud of him?

- If your manager treated you the way you treat your teen, how long would you remain at the job?

A policeman walked up to me at a mall in Tulsa, Oklahoma, when I was 13 years old and asked me if I stole any of the record albums in my hands. The mere fact that he asked the questions made me feel as if he was accusing me. So I gave a smart-aleck response to deflect any appearance of wrongdoing: "Heck, no!"

He responded, "I knew you were going to say that, so let me ask you again. Did you buy all those albums?"

After a little hesitation, I gave him my answer.

The first question was tough to swallow because of the sense of surprise, the feeling of being caught. But his second question allowed me to focus on the truth. My encouragement to you is to read the questions to parents in this section a second time. Why? Because even the smallest amount of wrongdoing on your part can ruin a relationship with your teen, just as a small drop of poison placed in a lake can kill all the fish in it.

Once I got over my surprise in that mall in Tulsa, I answered the policeman's second question:

"Nope."

Chapter 11

Another Downside of Divorce

■ ■ ■ ■

meet new friends every day. I travel and get out and about every week, and I am always trying to get in front of new people, so I spend quite a bit of time introducing myself to inquisitive new contacts. I've never been hesitant to tell people about my wife and me, our kids, our grandkids, our dogs, waterskiing, and the things that are currently happening in our lives.

When my son was going through his divorce, I would mention this to people in my introductory comments, and inevitably they would ask, "Did your son have any kids?" I was asked that question so many times that a little voice in the back of my head began whispering to me that maybe he did and I didn't know about them! I was asked this question 20 or 30 times. I'd tell them no, and their reaction was always a one-word remark: "Good." They knew what I see every day—divorce has a detrimental effect on kids.

Aaron came to us from a drug rehab program when my son was going through his divorce and I was being asked that question. I had the honor of including Aaron in my small group of new residents at Heartlight. Upon their arrival, the new "recruits" tell their story and share their reflections about how they got to Heartlight, what was going on in their lives, and what their issues have been. Aaron was comfortable with group meetings because of his stint in drug rehab, and when I asked him to share his life story, these were the first words out of his mouth: "I think it all started when my parents got a divorce. I was eight." Half the kids in the room agreed in a mumbling array of responses, with one girl saying, "You got that right!"

Aaron had walked home from school in the second grade to find his dad leaning against his car with all his belongings inside. He could tell that his dad had been crying. Aaron said that everything started going in slow motion as he listened to his dad say that he was moving out, that he and Mom were getting a divorce, and that he would get to see him on some weekends. Aaron didn't cry. He said it was kind of weird not to cry and break down sobbing and then he made a statement that has stuck with me for years. He said, "Instead of crying a whole bunch at once, I just cried one tear a day for the next eight years." Aaron recalled a time when he was 12 and his dad told him that they got to spend every other weekend together, as if that was plenty of time. But Aaron said he was thinking, *Yeah, but that's only four or six days a month. If you ate only six days a month, you'd be starving every other day.*

Amazing insight, isn't it?

Aaron was the class clown in his elementary school years, getting in trouble for talking and rarely receiving awards for scholastic performance. Teacher's meetings, disciplinary discussions, and educational testing sent the message that Aaron was a misfit with problems. Then he stated that there was one day that changed his life. (If you're a teacher reading this, pay attention to the power behind the words you say.) Aaron's teacher, a young lady who was frustrated with his behavior, made a statement to Aaron in front of the whole class that has echoed in his head ever since. She simply said, "If you weren't so stupid, maybe you wouldn't be in trouble all the time."

When Aaron came home that afternoon, he didn't mention a word about the teacher's comment, but he thought about it until he went to sleep that night…and every night for the next few years. When he got home that afternoon, he didn't have a dad at home to counteract the negative influence of that unwise teacher. He didn't have a dad at home that afternoon to reaffirm the value of his son's life. He didn't have a dad at soccer practice that day to cheer him on and let him know that he was a good kid, that he had someone in his cheering section, and that he was loved at the time he most needed to hear those three special words. He didn't have a dad at the dinner table that night to ask him how his day was, so he never had an opportunity to share what really happened that day.

That day was pivotal in Aaron's life, and he lived through it all by himself. A dad would have known what to do. Instead of blurting out his hurt, he stuffed his feelings and allowed negative thoughts and words to control his thoughts and image of himself.

No one should have been surprisesd when Aaron took the various drugs he was offered at school. They covered the negative thoughts he had carried about himself for so many years. He told me that eighth grade was a good year for him. It was the year he started using and finally felt relief from all the pain he carried from his feelings of abandonment and feeling stupid.

Aaron's mother remarried when he was in the seventh grade. He was reminded of the loss of his dad every morning when he ate breakfast with his new stepdad. Regardless of what the new stepdad did, his presence only reminded Aaron of what he was missing. So Aaron never got along with him. His stepfather's presence in the home reminded him of what he had lost, what he would never have again, and how things would have been different if his mom and dad had stayed together. When his mom remarried, Aaron knew that his mom and dad would never get back together, and he finally had to give up the fantasy.

School was tough on Aaron too. School was about academics, and Aaron was about socialization. His learning disabilities made academics hard, but he made up for it in personality. When school became too hard, he quit. And it wasn't because he didn't try. He just couldn't do it. To make matters worse, the older Aaron got, the less tolerant his youth minister and volunteer youth workers became of his clowning-around. Aaron had developed himself as the public funny guy to ease and hide all the pain inside. During the ninth grade, he was told he wasn't welcome on the summer mission trip because they needed to take people who were serious about God. That was when Aaron just gave up.

Now he was just labeled as rebellious and out of line. He really wanted to keep it all together, and when he realized he couldn't, he resorted to vices that calmed those inner voices of shame and countered his own thoughts of being worthless. The feelings of being rejected by his dad, teased by classmates because of his learning disabilities, humiliated by a teacher's loose lips, and excluded from the only place he felt accepted—his youth group—culminated in a drug habit that brought temporary peace to a life he didn't understand or want to accept.

I'm not making a judgment on divorce here. I won't enter into a discussion of the rights and wrongs, pros and cons, or good reasons and not-good-enough reasons for divorce. What happens between two people is really none of my business. I can give a lot of advice about marriage. I've been married 33 years and have a wonderful wife whom I have been happily married to for about 27 years. (The other six were the ones that bonded us together.) Anyway, I don't pass judgment about divorce. But I do speak about the effects that divorce has on kids. I can't help but believe that if a dad had been more visible and present in the early years of Aaron's life, much of the crud Aaron encountered along the way could have been countered by his dad's wise and loving words. Aaron is a good kid who felt abandoned and who attempted to stop the pain. Aaron needed someone to step in and counter all those wrong messages that played over and over in his head.

Jesus speaks to Aaron and all those who are hurting, abandoned, or rejected when He says, "Come to me, all you who are weary and burdened, and I will give you rest" (Matthew 11:28). He is a father to the fatherless, a friend to the friendless, and someone to lean on when everyone else has fallen down. He is the one who loves the unlovable and comforts those in need. He is the one who gives meaning to the hurts and reaches out with two arms to embrace those who feel as if they can't take any more. I pray daily for young people like Aaron, and I pray that God will continue to bring these young people into my life.

Do you have a son like this? Does this story sound familiar? Let me give you some ways you can reenter your teen's life and still be involved in a mighty way.

Work for Inclusion Rather Than Exclusion

Teens who have experienced divorce in their family feel left out. When parents split, the teens' lives split, and they're no longer whole. And when many parents remarry, teens feel as if they are on their own. In their minds, the parents who came together to create them have now gone two different ways and connected with others. It's a time of exclusion, and the older the children are when the separation happens, the more they feel the disconnect.

I encourage all parents in this situation to try extra hard to help their teen feel included rather than excluded. If a teen feels excluded, he will act on that feeling. Counter it. Invite him in even when an invitation doesn't seem necessary. Display pictures of your teen with you. Double the number of times that you tell your teen you love him, even when he's acting in a way that makes him hard to love. Let him know that he is still part of a family. If he doesn't feel like he has a family with you, he will find one or make one elsewhere.

Admit Fault

Did you make a mistake early on in your marriage? If so, then admit it so that your fault can't continually be used against you. If a parent doesn't accept this responsibility, a teen sometimes feels the need to prove the parent wrong and begins to work hard to make sure the parent pays for the mistake (and then some). Teens may purposely try to make it hard for you in a coercive attempt to move you to the point of admission. Let your teen know that you know your actions have hurt him. Just say it.

That doesn't mean you let him use that admission against you and manipulate and extort you. Teens will do that as well. As I've said many times, two wrongs don't make a right. Your admission of wrongdoing doesn't give license for him to do wrong.

Support the New Stepparent

Supporting your new spouse, the stepparent in your home, may be really tough in front of your teen. Supporting the stepparent on your former spouse's side is even tougher. That person may be the one your ex had an affair with. Or she may be the kindest person in the world. Your support of your child's stepparents may be difficult, but it will make it easier for your teen in the long run. Bite your tongue, pray for patience, put on a smile, and ask for strength. You don't lose and your ex doesn't win if your teen gets along with the new stepparent. You all win. So for the sake of your daughter, give her what she needs, not what your ex deserves.

Be There More

Even if you feel as if you're involved as much as you can be in your teen's life, if you are the noncustodial parent, double your efforts. If you only get every other weekend, ask for more. If you can't get it, see if you can meet your teen for lunch—grab a snack after school, make it to all her games or school programs, and get online in the evenings and exchange messages on MySpace or Facebook. Instant message her just to say hi, and text her to say "I love you."

Let your daughter know you desire to be involved in her life. The amount of time you give her transfers a level of value that no one else can give. If she doesn't get it from you, she will get it from someone else, and it won't be anywhere close to the quality of value that you can transfer.

Stick Around If You Haven't Split Yet

I have grown to think the world of those couples who, knowing that they're going to get divorced, hang in there together until their teens graduate from high school (if they can live together in a mature and amicable arrangement). I know that many different arguments can be made about that statement, but people would have a tough time convincing me that a child is better off with parents living in separate homes. The couple may be better off, but not the child. Sons need their moms. Daughters need their dads. Sons need their dads. Daughters need their moms. Would you consider staying around until your teen is independent?

I'm not saying that divorce causes all the problems in the life of a child, but I am saying that divorce causes damage and piles the stuff in a child's life a little higher. Also, consider the opportunity cost attached to the split. It's an opportunity cost very few people think about—all the opportunities you and your child will miss when you can't be together.

Chapter 12

The Problem with Perfection:
Quiet Rebellion Behind a Pretty Face

■ ■ ■ ■

Most people think of a rebellious teen as one who is wild and crazy, self-centered and self-absorbed, indignant and disrespectful, spinning out of control, full of arguments and cussing, always yelling and screaming. Right? Well, Laura wasn't that way. I walked in the room to meet her, and there sat a well-mannered young lady who greeted me and answered all my questions with a "No, sir" or "Yes, sir." She was cordial, nice, engaging, and very personable. She answered every question perfectly. We were interviewing her to make the decision whether she should leave home and come live at Heartlight, and everything seemed perfect. But was it?

As I sat with her parents and they shared about their daughter, they told me everything that was right and nothing that was wrong. After a couple of hours of listening to how perfect life was for this family, I had to ask, "Why are we sitting here talking about having your daughter leave home if everything is so perfect?" Tears fell as they began to share how Laura had become defiant almost overnight. They told me how she was sneaking out at night to meet her new boyfriend. He was a "problem kid" who "just wasn't Laura's type." She never screamed at her parents about it, but she kept ignoring their directives and rules. She never yelled or responded in anger; she just did what she wanted, sneaking around and acting as if she didn't care about what they said. Her mom described it as a quiet rebellion.

They shared how she had gone on every mission trip at the church, but recently she had been sending suggestive pictures of herself over the Internet. They talked of how compliant she has always been, making straight A's in school, and how she was now lying to them about where she was really going on her way home from school or when she ran errands for them. Mom talked about how Laura had been the perfect child before, but now she heard Laura cussing over the phone. Dad talked about all the sports that she had been involved in before and how hard it was recently to find her having sex in her boyfriend's car in front of their house.

When I asked them if they really felt she needed to leave home to get away from this boyfriend, her dad told me he thought God could use her in the lives of the other kids at Heartlight. Since that didn't really answer my question, he then asked his wife what she thought. She commented that she thought Heartlight was the perfect place for her daughter. The thing that concerned me the most was that everything was so "perfect." Well, we did take Laura into our program because she did need to get away from her home environment and make some changes in her life. I soon saw that an imperfect person doesn't function well in a "perfect" world.

After Laura came to live with us, her parents called and e-mailed constantly about little things that were wrong with our operation. They explained, in a very nice way, that our staff didn't handle something right, or the meals weren't really that good, or one of the staff members was going a couple of miles per hour over the speed limit. They told us that the plants on the property needed to be watered more. They told us that we should try a different feed for the horses. They questioned the purpose of everything we did, and they did it in a way that really grated on me. They demanded perfection with a smile. They let us know that the house Laura moved into was too cold at night and that the girls didn't have enough hot water for showers. (Do they ever?)

Eventually, whenever I saw their number on my phone, I ignored it, hoping that they wouldn't call so much. I became mute on the phone with them, listening, letting whatever they said go in one ear and out the other. They e-mailed me questions, but I wouldn't answer them. Whatever I said wouldn't be good enough. Other staff members who were in communication with them began to feel the same and shared that regardless of how hard they tried, it was never good enough.

At one of our family retreats, where we asked all parents to participate, all I could do while I was with them following our introductory chit-chat was smile and nod as I listened to their barrage of comments and questions. They used me as their sounding board in their quest for perfection. I ignored them the whole time they were in our presence; I didn't want to talk with them, and secretly, in my heart of hearts, I didn't think many good thoughts about them.

They were always on time—down to the second. They looked perfect when they arrived. Their rental car never got dirty. Their son, Laura's younger brother, was perfect every time we saw him. Their shoes were always shined, their clothes always matched, and I don't think they ever perspired. Incredibly, they maintained a perfect appearance. As they sat in parent meetings, they focused on what was wrong with everyone else in the program rather than hearing the wisdom that was being shared to help them in their relationship with their daughter. They really felt that they didn't need any help. In their minds and words, they were perfect; their daughter was the one who needed the help. They even mentioned that they were having a tough time understanding how Laura could do so wrong, when they were doing everything so right.

The week following one of the retreats, I was sitting on my back porch having a cup of coffee, praying and thinking through our relationship with them. As if a light was suddenly turned on, I thought, *These parents are doing to me exactly what they have been doing to Laura.* Laura's and my response to her parents were the same. Their pull on Laura was the same pull they were having on me, and it was having the same effect on our relationship with one another. I wanted them to go away, not because some of their comments and criticisms were true (no one is perfect) but because of the way they approached people and arrogantly presented themselves. They wouldn't go away, so I did.

They were correct in some of their criticisms and observations, but that wasn't the point. They really weren't critical people, but they were on a quest for perfection. And since they felt as if they had attained that high honor, they were determined to make sure that everyone else in their circle did the same. That's when I knew how to approach Laura to get her to start talking.

As I shared my observations with her, I could tell I hit a nerve when I talked about never being good enough. I ventured into my observations about her parents, and knew that I was plowing into some untilled soil. I shared how they made me feel. I shared my reaction and how I wanted to avoid them. Tears streamed down her face as she asked, "You mean I'm not crazy?" I told her that she wasn't, but we couldn't allow her to continue negative behavior patterns that could destroy her life. I assured her that we were going to help her break some of the perfection patterns that she was demonstrating in her own life.

Laura's parents thought that the negative changes they saw in their daughter happened overnight. But they didn't happen that way at all. Her movement toward an imperfect world was a slow, uncalculated drift away from a fantasy world of perfection that didn't exist and would never come to pass this side of heaven. Her parents thought everything changed overnight, but it had been a long time coming. The crowning blow that tipped the scales was an argument about the way Laura should wear her hair. Laura was tired of maintaining a facade of perfection because she knew she wasn't perfect. The hair incident just happened to be the catalyst that allowed all of Laura's frustration to become visible. Her parents had long been blind to the growing anger and frustration boiling in the life of their daughter, who had always been expected to put on a happy face.

Dealing with a teen who speaks her mind, cusses you out, and displays a hatred and disdain for what you are trying to accomplish in her life is difficult. But even worse is a teen who is smiling and presenting herself as having it all together when truly, everything is falling apart. At least I know where a teen stands when she spews. I can't be so sure about the one who is just as rebellious but doesn't give me a clue as to what she might be thinking or what she wants from life. Laura was a smiler, a teen who covered up her rage with a beautiful smile and a winsome personality. But deep down in her heart she was miserable, and that misery was beginning to leak out all over her life.

Many parents who have smilers demanded perfection and justified their position with Matthew 5:48, which states, "Be perfect, therefore, as your heavenly Father is perfect." What many don't realize is that this verse has to do with how one is to approach an enemy, *not* how parents are to run their lives, manage their household, or raise their kids. A perfectionist parent sends a message to a teen that something good can never happen in the presence of something bad. In this mind-set, the absence of difficulty and struggle denotes a better life than one where both are present. If these two things are true, then struggle, hurt, mistakes, failure, and sin are best ignored and avoided.

This poses a quandary for anyone living in a teen world, where life is full of struggle, hurt, mistakes, failure, and sin. When we ignore that part of a teen's life, we force him to find empathy and sympathy from others and turn to others for the answers he is not receiving at home. The perfectionist mind-set creates the conditions for the perfect storm, and teens often think perfection is what their parents want and expect from them. This creates a lot more problems than you might think, and it damages many more relationships than you might think. Really, all families, especially Christian families, have a touch of the perfectionist mind-set. Sometimes it's called "high standards," sometimes "doing your best," and sometimes "being a good witness or example." Whatever you label it, kids hear this message: "You must be perfect." If that is true, all families must counter the effects of what their teen thinks they are being told.

Laura's family is an extreme example of this perfectionist mind-set. Your child might not have reacted to the extent that Laura did, but her example provides a good lesson for all families.

We all want the best for our kids. We never want anything bad to happen to them. And we really do want them to fulfill every bit of their unique purpose. But they also need to know that perfection isn't possible. Lots of things can go wrong, Santa isn't real, the Tooth Fairy doesn't leave money under the pillow, and the Easter Bunny doesn't really bring the eggs.

When children are in the early elementary school years, they do believe, for the most part, that life can be good and perfect. Parents are superheroes. Mom and Dad can do no wrong in the eyes of most young children. Young children don't think about looks, weight, possessions, or popularity. Life is practically perfect. It's the only time that kids will give their moms and dads shirts that say "Super Dad" or "Super Mom" and run to greet their heroes as soon as they walk in the door.

Then adolescence comes along, and children's eyes are opened to how imperfect the world really is—and how imperfect the people around them are. Training has to be constant, and parents have to make daily deposits into the life of their child. Think of it like exercise. It would be nice if a big deposit of exercise in the high school and college years would pay off with a nice, toned body for the rest of our lives. But it doesn't work that way. Neither can parents store up their training deposits. Many parents believe that what they taught and conveyed during their child's earlier years will carry them through their adolescent years. This is simply not true. Exercise over a long period of time yields good results, and the same is true with the training of a child. You can't quit training because you think you've trained a perfect child (based solely on her perfect responses). Instead, you need to shift your training style to accommodate the changing needs of your teen as she walks through her imperfect adolescent world.

Romans 3:23 says, "For all have sinned and fall short." This is a verse that is usually used as an evangelistic tool to share with people their need for Christ. This verse also makes me feel better about myself. My own depravity and shortcomings don't isolate me from everyone else. It's a good reminder, truly, that we all fall short. No perfect kids, no perfect parents. Whew! Isn't that a relief?

We do well to build our kids' self-confidence and self-esteem, telling them, "You're the best," "You're all winners!" "You're a princess!" and "You da man!" But we also have to prepare them for the day when they realize they're really not the best, they're not princesses, and hundreds of other budding adolescents have also been told, "You da man." If we don't, they might feel as if their "perfect" mom and dad sold them a perfect bill of goods, and they're no longer going to buy it.

This was the process Laura went through. When she discovered that her new adolescent world was not like the world her parents had described and still tried to live in, Laura tried to cope with her feelings of imperfection, and she began to express her anger and disappointment in the best way she knew how. Some would call it passive-aggressiveness. Others might label it as an inward rage masked by a happy face. I would call it the "perfect" result of a perfectionist mind-set and message.

It's a dangerous message to send to teens. A perfectionist mind-set and message calls for self-reliance rather than dependence on God. It forces people to try to create a world that will never exist rather than a lifestyle that relies on the salvation of Christ and the presence of the Holy Spirit in the midst of the struggles of everyday life. No wonder kids raised under a perfectionist mind-set rebel! They don't want to live like mom and dad want them to and rebel in order to break out of the illusion of perfection.

So what are parents to do when they realize that they have expected perfection? Simply communicate how life really is and maintain dialogue as your teen realizes what life really looks like—a sinful mess at times. That's when grace comes in and salvation becomes real. Perfect people don't need to be saved from anything. When you know you are basically a train wreck, you're more likely to understand your need to be rescued by the love of God. That's what Laura eventually found through her struggle and her eventual acceptance of her imperfections—a need to ask Jesus for a place of comfort and a reassurance that she was loved in her imperfection.

Parents, is it important for your teen to be perfect? If so, why? Could your demand for perfection be driving your teen to embrace a world of imperfection? If everything is so perfect, why are you struggling with your teen? Could a struggling teen be a reflection of your "perfect" parenting skills? Just ask. Some of the most rebellious teens I see come from "perfect" homes. Evidently something isn't all that perfect.

Chapter 13

Life's Tough When You're Stupid

■ ■ ■ ■

was born in Midland, Texas. I lived there for a whole ten days. My dad was on an oil-blasting seismograph crew, and I guess the truck just happened to be parked in that oil town when my mom had me. When asked where I'm from, I tell people I was born in Texas, I was raised in southern Louisiana, I lived in Tulsa, and I grew up after I got married. Now I call Longview, Texas, home. I'm proud to be a Texan. I love horses and a good pair of boots. I own too many guns, and a few cowboy hats, and I have used the same set of spurs for 20 years. I love the best lines in John Wayne movies. When you're around horses, you quickly learn the definition of courage attributed to him: "Courage is being scared to death but saddling up anyway." And the line I remember most is one he said as the character Sergeant Striker in the movie *The Sands of Iwo Jima*: "Life is tough, but it's tougher when you're stupid."

Life is hard for teens today. Our tough culture will eat them alive if they're struggling. And life will be even harder if they do something stupid. Many times, parents interpret stupid acts as forms of rebellion when those acts really aren't signs of rebellion at all. They're merely stupid acts. But how parents respond to those stupid acts might determine whether their teen kicks into a form of rebellion.

When I was six years old, I heard my first rock 'n' roll song by Buddy Holly—"That'll Be the Day." The song title was inspired by

John Wayne's constant use of the phrase in the 1956 epic *The Search-ers*. I was hooked on this new type of music the minute I heard it. I bought the 45-rpm and played it until I wore the needle off of my turntable.

When I was nine years old, I spent the night with a friend across the street from where I lived. His mother, Mrs. Lovingfoss, decided to take us down to City Park Stadium in New Orleans to see a rock band that had come to town. It was September 16, 1964, and the band was from Liverpool, England. I stood at an iron fence and watched this band play the same songs I heard on WNOE-FM or WTIX-FM at night. I loved it. As we drove away from the concert, it started to rain, and I kept singing over and over in my head, "I want to hold your hand." I sang it so much that fourth grade year that three other guys and I got suspended from school for impersonating the Beatles during recess. (Can you believe that?)

I was crazy about music in the '60s. Watching shows like ABC's *Shindig!* NBC's *Hullabaloo*, and Dick Clark's *American Bandstand* only fueled my addiction to it. I listened to it at night on a transistor radio, wrote the names of bands on my school notebook, and fell in love with rock 'n' roll. I listened to Jimi Hendrix and Janis Joplin, and I even got to see The Doors in concert back in the early days. I was crazy for the Beach Boys and dreamed of living in California. As a matter of fact, I accepted Christ at a Beach Boys concert, where Dave Wilkerson came out at intermission and preached. (Top that!) I helped the group Chicago unload a bus when they performed in Tulsa when I was in ninth grade. When John Denver hit the scene, I wanted to move to the Rocky Mountains and play guitar. I was a fan of Ricky Nelson, and I even got to see Elvis in concert the year before he died. My first date with my wife, Jan, was to a Led Zeppelin concert. Music, for me, was a great pastime, but I became a little concerned when I heard about my idols' lifestyles.

All the bands or individuals I've mentioned have experienced some sort of tragedy that resulted in a death of someone in the band or the individual. I won't go into all the details or pass judgment on their debacles, but I will say that most of the people who died were more stupid than they were rebellious.

I do know this. When I go see the remnants of these groups perform today, I am touched deeply as I watch the ones who survived. I see them on stage and think back to when I first heard their songs. Rarely does a performance go by that I don't tear up a little, thinking about how cool it is that these last members of the groups are survivors, perhaps of their own stupidity. At the same time, I have a sense of loss that many who used to perform with them are no longer around. Many. Just because of stupid mistakes.

I know that I have done just as many stupid things as they have. And only by the grace of God am I still on the face of this earth. As odd as it may sound, when I go to concerts, see people who were performing 40 years ago, and hear them singing those old songs, I have sort of a worship experience. I nostalgically think of the loss while wonderfully embracing the goodness of these people's lives now. God has protected so many in the midst of their stupidity, and I stand in awe of how God has protected me in spite of my own stupidity.

I've done some pretty stupid stuff. I've been fired from jobs and handled that badly, and I have fired others wrongly. I've offended people I didn't intend to and offended people I did intend to. I have said things that were better off left unsaid. I have not sought counsel before making decisions and then regretted it. I have yelled at people when I should have remained soft. I have been extremely selfish, and I have many thoughts that the world should revolve around me. I have been unappreciative of what others have done for me, and I have been clueless about what many have sacrificed. I've been disobedient, disrespectful, and occasionally dishonest. I have not listened when I should have, said things when I shouldn't, and refrained from saying things when I should have. I've lost some good friends because of my stupidity, and I have done some stupid things with some not-so-good friends. I have sought vengeance and prayed for revenge. I have acted in anger and walked away from people when I should have walked toward them. I haven't always practiced what I preached, and I haven't always followed good counsel. I burned down a lady's wooden fence, took a tractor from a construction site and drove it into a pond, turned a guy's car upside down in the school parking lot, and stole a 12-foot plastic cow mounted on a trailer and drove it down a street until it popped off our trailer hitch. And I never went back to see where that cow ended up.

I've done some pretty stupid stuff. Just like your teen. Perhaps just like you.

Carl was 15 years old when he pulled a couple of stupid stunts. He got drunk for the first time while spending the night at his friend's house. A liquor cabinet was open, and the two boys' curiosity got the best of them. Carl threw up all over the cloth couch at his friend's house and then fell asleep, and his mistake left a mark that his friend's mother was pretty upset about.

His second blunder was when he lit a Roman candle on the school bus and held it out the window while riding home on the last day of school. His poor choice of celebration led to his arrest. Charges were eventually dropped and chalked up to juvenile stupidity. The judge snickered at his shenanigans; his father didn't. Dad grounded him for the entire summer, made him work on their farm, and told him that he couldn't get his license until he was 17.

I believe in consequences. But I believe that they must be fair because too bold of a stand might just push a young man into a rebellion that could have been prevented. That's what happened to Carl. His junior year in high school was a mess, for now he was an angry young man who couldn't shake the two stupid acts he committed a few months earlier. His dad would not let them go. His behavior spun out of control, he dropped out of school, and he moved in with a buddy who was off at college.

I honestly believe that if Carl's dad had handled Carl's stupid acts a little differently, Carl could have rebounded from his mistakes and carried on a normal life. Too many times, parents throw gasoline on the fires teens start, rather than dousing those hotspots with living water. Mishandling of stupid stunts can turn them into an inferno, burning the bridges for a child to remain at home. Carl never went back.

How parents respond to their teen's occasional stupid stunts is important. I encourage parents to remember all the stunts they pulled growing up before they respond to their son or daughter. And I remind them that God is at work in the life of their teen just as much as He is involved in theirs. Life's tougher when you're stupid. Let the natural consequences of stupid acts occur, and remember your youth, the times you were caught and the times you weren't. One day you'll laugh at the stunts your teen pulled, just as much as you sit back and laugh at the stunts you pulled. Go easy on your teen if it's just a one-time deal. You were once that age too, weren't you?

Chapter 14

Going to a Princess Brawl

■ ■ ■ ■

Three years ago, as I walked with my daughter, granddaughter, and some friends along the Strand in Hermosa Beach, California, I was reminded of the "princess world" my granddaughter was growing up in. As she looked at the black concrete that sparkled in the street lights, she looked up to me with wonderment in her eyes and said, "Poppa, look at the sparkles on the ground. Is this fairy dust from Tinkerbell?"

The question stopped me in my tracks and reminded me of how innocent she still was—and how that innocence of childhood would be lost in just a few short years. Her fairy tale–filled heart wanted to believe that she had encountered a true glimpse of a fantasy world that made her feel special. And I wanted to believe that, for just a moment, she would experience something innocent and true, knowing that she would one day learn that the world can be quite different from a fairy tale.

She and so many other girls under 12 years old have been raised in a fantasy world where princesses exist and where they are princesses too. Parents give them princess lunch boxes, buy them princess T-shirts, put princess pillowcases and blankets on their beds, and let them play princess games on the computer. Girls have princess-themed birthday parties, and some parents even take their little princesses to the wonderful world of Disney to get a firsthand look at a princess kingdom.

Parents lead the way from one attraction to the next, snapping pictures of the Disney princesses with their little princess.

Daddies tell their daughters they are "little princesses" and want them to know how special they are, how unique they are, and how beautiful they are. I understand that some granddads, ahem, buy their granddaughters princess outfits to enhance the feeling of being beautiful and good, trying to take advantage of the age of innocence before the little girls grow up.

This commercialized "princess thinking" has convinced hundreds of thousands of young girls that they are, indeed, princesses. Parents communicate that nothing is too good for their little princess, so they buy her everything. Many idolize their daughters, dressing them up to show off how beautiful and wonderful they are. Dads wear "My daughter is a princess" T-shirts. Daughters confirm this by wearing "I'm Daddy's little princess" T-shirts. Other parents will rotate their lives around their daughter, doing anything for her, going everywhere with her, and taking pictures, making scrapbooks, and memorializing everything she does to value her and let her know how special she is.

A princess is a ruler of a principality, and a sovereign female. Many countries have only one. Rarely do two exist in the same place, much less hundreds all converging on the same place to start middle school. It doesn't take much to understand why little girls' battles with each other begin. They compete for territory, boundaries, position, and retention of the crown.

Erika was one of those princesses. Her dad was one of those T-shirt totin' knights in shining armor who proudly displayed the position of his little princess in the words on his chest. With a great sense of healthy pride he wore that shirt on Saturdays when he hung out with his daughter. He spent countless hours letting her know she was loved and cared for and held a special place in her daddy's heart. Nothing was wrong with calling his daughter a princess, for she was.

Erika knew it. She knew deep in her heart how much she was loved and cared for. Her understanding of her place in her dad's heart led her to believe that the crown she wore was secure. Make no mistake, mom was the queen, but Erika was the princess, second in line to the throne. She was important, loved, probably a little spoiled (as are all good princesses), and cherished. Consequently, her transition from monarch to one of many ordinary citizens was not easy.

Lindsey wasn't raised in a home where she was the princess. Her mom and dad divorced when she was four, and she always felt that her bloodline was tainted. She would never become royalty like the other girls. Lindsey longed for a T-shirt totin' dad who proclaimed his allegiance to his princess. One day in fifth grade, after a softball practice and as she waited for her mom to pick her up, she watched a few of the dads patting their princesses on the back, wearing the "My daughter is my princess" T-shirt, and telling their girls that they'd stop for a snow cone after practice.

Lindsey said that watching the other girls made her feel lonely because no dad patted her back or wore a shirt about her. While most of the girls drove off in a "carriage," she felt as if her queen drove a pumpkin, and her afternoon agenda included household chores, not snow cones with a knight in shining armor. Her knight's armor was tarnished, and he never seemed interested in this little princess's heart.

Lindsey's dad commented on all the good things he saw in her on the occasional times he did see her, but those times seemed to be waning, and his words didn't carry the same weight now that he had remarried and had a new little princess. Her mother, the queen, was searching for a new king, her dad was now a ruler in a faraway land, and Lindsey felt lost and alone in the now-divided kingdom. This was confirmed when she saw her dad wearing one of those shirts— one that proclaimed his "new" daughter was his princess. That shirt sealed the deal on a deteriorating relationship that to Lindsey seemed obligatory and insincere.

As Lindsey's eyes opened more and more to her situation, she began to feel a rage inside her little heart. She was just as worthy to be a princess as any of the other princesses she had seen. And with the upcoming move to middle school, she was ready to break out of her pauper status and pursue her God-given right to rule. She wanted what others had and what she had been denied. And she was bound and determined to get it. Welcome to the princess brawl!

Erika chose "mean girl madness" as a way to preserve the princess position she had been rightly given. Lindsey opted for "girl-on-girl bullying" to attain the princess position she had been wrongly denied. It was a fight for princess pecking order that would determine position and value.

At the first day of middle school, the princesses usually greet one another, size up the opponents, and start to form a silent battle strategy. Alliances are made, battlegrounds are determined, and phone numbers and e-mail addresses are exchanged. If I had a nickel for every time parents have told me how their cute little princess went off to middle school one day and returned that afternoon a different person, I'd be rich. The fireworks usually begin on the second day of school.

Most of these girls use their words and their appearance as their two main weapons. They cut the other princesses down with a verbal barrage of cruel comments. The old saying "Sticks and stones may break my bones, but words will never hurt me" is a half-truth. The words hurled back and forth in conversations between girls are cutthroat and can be horrible. The negative impact of these hateful words can damage a tender heart for years.

Many little princesses use words to destroy image and reputations and to damage self-confidence as they have a verbally charged game of "king of the hill." Technology today intensifies and multiplies the cruel insults. I call it "digital courage." Girls use text messaging, e-mails, chat rooms, social networks, and instant messaging behind a veil of invisibility to unleash their evil attacks.

The second strategy for positioning and winning over the masses is to utilize one's appearance to draw attention, thus winning the popularity vote. This is especially important in the life of teens, just as it was when we were growing up. Teens care how they look. One of the most difficult aspects for today's teen girls is the growing influence and push to present themselves sexually. The demands for sexual presentation that once were limited to college and high school girls have now trickled down to the junior high and middle school girls.

By the time girls enter their middle school years, they possess just about everything because knights in shining armor (dads) have lavished them with gifts. So if every girl has basically the same stuff, how is she supposed to show her individuality in a culture where identity is determined by what you have and what you don't have? The answer has become to present their physical attributes. Guys have not caused this, though they certainly haven't discouraged it. Pornography isn't solely to blame, although that hasn't helped either.

By the time girls enter middle school, they want to appear older than they are. They feel as if they need to one-up the other princesses. The sexual influence in the teen culture adds fuel to the flame, pushing our young girls to take a walk on the wilder side in hopes of securing a higher position among their princess peers.

The digital world allows the transfer of pictures almost instantaneously. It's becoming commonplace to talk about sexual issues and to transfer sexual images through cell phones. Girls display seductive pictures of themselves on Internet social networking sites. Young men who once received notes in class now receive seductive pictures of girls through their cell phones. And if the girl doesn't have the goods to attract attention, image-altering software on a computer can enhance any photo. In a guy's visually stimulated makeup, the images fuel the sexiness of conversation and move some guys to request more from these princesses.

Times have changed, haven't they? I find myself shaking my head in disbelief and thinking, *Can you believe that?* when I hear of new antics kids are up to and when I hear how young these kids are when the antics begin. I'm old enough to remember when television stations went off the air at night, but that doesn't mean I'm too old to adapt to the needs of a girl who is struggling through these princess brawls. Every parent must get to know and try to understand the changing teen culture. Parents must be aware of their child's response to that new culture if they want to maintain the wonderful connection they had with their child in her younger years.

When your teen comes home from school and is angry, distraught, confused, lost, and full of hate for everything she once loved, she may not be rebelling at all. She might be coming home as a war-torn soldier who has been engaging in battle all day. And the fact that she takes out her frustration on the knight in now-tarnished armor (dad) or the queen of the castle (mom) doesn't mean she doesn't love them anymore. It may mean that these are the only two people who still know her as she really is…a true princess in need of love from the knight and queen.

Most perceived rebellion is really a response to outside forces in a teen's life. This is key to determining a parent's appropriate and effective response to a princess's inappropriate behavior. Mom and Dad, please don't come down too hard on distasteful behavior. She may be simply reacting now. But you could inadvertently push her to true rebellion.

Your little princess may be coming home every day exhausted from a day of battling to keep the crown you placed on her head. Or she may be trying to win a crown she so rightly deserves. Both are exhausting, and she may have good intentions. However, the ways girls engage in this "mean world" usually are not good. And this culture isn't helping them in any way; it's accelerating the exposure that is stealing our children's childhood. Erika and Lindsey are good kids caught in a world that is very confusing, and they need a knight in shining armor who brings light into their darkness and allows their own light to shine in spite of many other princess's attempts to snuff it out.

So which one is your daughter? Is she trying to maintain the crown you proudly handed her? Or is she desperately trying to be crowned because of the attention she did not receive? The behavior looks the same.

Parents can do a number of things to help alleviate princess brawls and reduce the amount of collateral damage these little princesses-turned-warriors can cause. You can't completely stop the wars, but you can curb much of the violence, counter the attacks, and restore respect.

Curb the Violence

An understanding of the world your little princess lives in goes a long way in tempering your response to your daughter, whether she is the aggressor or the recipient of others' aggression. Be prepared. And if princess drama does not affect your child, consider yourself blessed. Perhaps your battles will be in other arenas. Still, play it smart. Here are some thoughts worth considering:

- Let you daughter know you will monitor her text messages, e-mails, and cameras. People live up to what you inspect, not what you expect, so assure her that you're going to be looking all the time.

- Report any harassment or Internet bullying to school officials or other parents. This may make you feel uncomfortable, but your reporting might keep the bullying from happening to others.

- Keep your daughter's cell phone in your name so you can have access to numbers and messages sent and received.

- Occasionally look at your teen's MySpace page and start clicking. What you find might give you some good conversation starters with her.

- Have a discussion with your daughter about your concern for what comes in her ears and what goes out of her mouth. The first tendency that most teens have when challenged by other kids is to engage and challenge back. But turnabout is not fair play in this game; it merely fuels the spark into a raging fire.

Counter the Attacks

When damage is done, anger and hurt are normal reactions. Usually when people are hurt, they respond with "fight or flight." They retaliate or retreat. Neither is better or worse; both are normal. Remember this when you determine your response. You can't always stop damage from happening, but you can create an atmosphere that counters the effects. Here are some pointers:

- Affirm, affirm, affirm. This is a time to console your child, not to tell her to clean her room, make straight A's, and feed the dog. Your teen has been wounded and needs some tenderness.

- Give positive messages in the form of notes and text messages.

- Buy her something when she isn't expecting it. Surprise her. Gifts are almost always welcomed.

- Get together once a week for breakfast or dinner and just sit and talk. Go to a movie that might stimulate some conversation. See a film about mean girls and plan a time to sit down and talk.

- Share about time when you have been hurt by friends. Let your daughter know she is not the only one who has been hurt or betrayed—not to belittle what she is going through, but to let her know she is not alone.

- Have Dad take the princess out for a special dinner at her favorite place. Don't just live off of memories from the past. Create new memories with special trips, experiences, and opportunities.

- Take your daughter and one of her friends on a weekend shopping trip. You might think you can't afford it, but maybe you can't afford not to.

Restore the Respect

I've never met a young lady or former princess who, having suffered the damage of some mean girls, is totally innocent of wrongdoing. There is usually some reason that meanness is aimed at a person. Let your daughter know that the greatest of all princesses is one who is a respecter of all people. Let this be the motto of your home: Respect all! Make sure your daughter understands the following:

- When someone hurts her, that doesn't give her an excuse to hurt someone back.

- You may understand her pain, but that doesn't make it okay for her to be disrespectful to anyone in the family.

- If she disrespects people through conversation, e-mail, chat rooms, or networking pages, you will talk about it, and consequences will follow.

- Pictures she takes and shares with others must be modest and not seductive.

- You understand the situation, but she has to refrain from retaliation. Regardless of how hard it is to bite her tongue, she must respect even when she is being disrespected.

I often see parents who raise their kids to live in a zoo rather than preparing them to survive in a jungle. We all know how animals raised in the zoo fare once they are released in the wild. They don't last long. Savvy parents have discussions with their child about the jungle and occasionally allow their child to wander in the safer spots of the jungle to get a glimpse of what might be lurking in the darkness. Actions like these tend to help daughters survive princess brawls.

My granddaughter and I were recently sitting down by the computer, looking at all the pictures I took of her with the princesses at Disney World. As she looked at all the pictures, Maile said, "Poppa, those are really just girls dressed up like princesses, aren't they?"

I told her, "Yeah, they're just girls."

She then asked, "Am I just like one of those girls, or am I really a princess?"

"Oh, sweetheart," I said, "you'll always be a princess."

Then I thought, *We've got to start getting her ready for battle. She's growing up way too fast.*

Chapter 15

Loving the Sinner Is Harder Than I Thought

■ ■ ■ ■

I was always told to hate the sin but love the sinner. That worked well as long as the sin wasn't one that bothered me and the sinner had already changed his ways. Some sins always seemed to be worse than others. And I was more prone to like a person once he had gotten on the good side of his sin and could talk about it in the past tense. To me, that made a relationship with a sinner a little more palatable, and it made the sinner a lot easier to love because I didn't have to deal with all the stuff that usually comes with sinners. I learned many, many years ago was that it was easy for me to love low-maintenance sinners; the higher-maintenance ones were a little more challenging. This came with my impression that I was a low-maintenance kind of guy. Birds of a feather flock together.

I used to tell people all the time that I loved them with the love of the Lord. I figured that I was not capable of loving them myself and that the love of the Lord was better than I could do on my own. Besides, it just sounded good. Truth be told, in my early years of working with families and kids, I'm not so sure that I loved them at all, at least until the sinner was no longer sinning and could tell a happy story about his conversion.

Kevin helped me learn what it means to truly love. Kevin was a young man who came to live with us, and the minute we met, I knew he was going to be one of those guys who's tough for us Texans to love.

His dress was stylish, his voice feminine, and his mannerisms a little uncomfortable to my macho style. He talked about things that were foreign to most of the other guys—cooking, trendy clothes, dancing, and photography. (Of course, nothing is wrong with those things.) Fortunately, he also liked to ride horses, so every time I saw that the other boys in our program were giving him a tough time, I gave him the signal to go saddle up a couple of horses, and we'd wander off into the piney woods. We talked about his life, his dreams, and his struggles while he cooled down a little.

Kevin's mother told me that his propensity toward feminine things was evident from the time he began to walk. He always wanted to be in the kitchen helping Mom. He loved playing with dolls. He loved to shop. And he didn't like to do guy things. I had several conversations with Kevin's mother about "nature versus nurture." Some guys seems to be born with more feminine characteristics than other guys, just as some girls (we used to call them tomboys) are born with more masculine characteristics than other girls.

I think we're all born with a "bent" of some sort, and that, coupled with choices we make in life, can take us to good places and bad places. My intent isn't to give a dissertation on the origins of homosexuality. My intent here is just to say that Kevin had some tendencies that had more to do with nature than with nurture.

But Kevin's mother did nurture this tendency. She took him to fashion shows, taught him to cook for Dad, and put him in dresses that she had hoped to one day be put on her anticipated daughter. She wouldn't allow him to get dirty, watch sports, or wear swimsuits like board shorts. He had to wear Speedo suits to the ridicule of all his friends, as early as the second grade. My point isn't that Speedo swimsuits are feminine. I wore them for 13 years when I swam competitively. The point is that this mom had a selfish desire to have her son do what she wanted him to do, even when it meant his friends made fun of him. Kevin was teased by everyone. It never stopped. If it wasn't one thing, it was another. By the time he came to live with us, he had been beaten up numerous times, called every name in the book, and shamed by most of his family members. People around this young man just couldn't back off. As a result, Kevin found no rest in his world.

His dad didn't help much either. In times of rage and anger over not getting the son he had hoped for, his father called him a fag, gay, queer, and girlie-boy. His dad told me, "He's my son, not my daughter," and he just couldn't get over his embarrassment of having his son strike up conversations in the kitchen with the women when friends visited. Kevin took notice of all this, and his dad's words and actions sent a clear message that there was never going to be any rest from the ridicule in his home.

When Kevin was 15, he went to church camp and prayed that God would change him. He shared his gut-wrenching prayers with me about how he hated who he was and how he wanted to be free from what he was being convinced was his old sin nature. He asked God to heal him from the damage of the past. He wanted to be born again so he could start over. He quoted Scripture: "Therefore, if anyone is in Christ, he is a new creation; the old has gone, the new has come!" (2 Corinthians 5:17). He anticipated a new life.

Then he had to go home.

Within the first week of returning from youth camp, the youth minister took him out to lunch and told him he needed to change the way he dressed. The youth leader also thought it would be best if Kevin didn't go on their annual mission trip because it would cause problems with the other guys. They were, in the youth minister's terms, uncomfortable around him. The pastor of the church called him in and asked that he not be so expressive when he sang in the youth choir, stating that his excitement made him stick out. Kevin wouldn't be invited to "afterglows," birthday parties, or special events. Kids couldn't give it a rest, and this kid couldn't find relief if it hit him in the face. What he did find was that the church he attended was just as critical of him as his family, his school, and people who didn't even know him.

I want to make sure that this is understood. At this point in Kevin's life, he repeatedly told me he was not gay. He had never participated in any homosexual behavior. He never said that he was attracted to same-sex relationships. And he never did anything that would justify the ridicule he received. This kid couldn't get a break. As I think back on our conversations, I'm sure he lived a life of torment, hurt, and confusion. I think all he wanted was some rest from the constant ridicule he received for something he didn't create, choose, or foster.

Eventually, the only time he could find some rest or get a break from the ridicule was when he was drunk. He explained to me that it was the only time he could get his mind off all the turmoil in his life and forget about what he hoped he was not. I was never in favor of his drinking behavior, but I certainly understood his motives. He wanted to find a way to survive. He wanted to be normal. He wanted to be different from who he was. And he was scared to death of the "G" word, fearing that he might not be who he wanted to be and that he may be what he didn't want to be. He told me over and over again that he was not gay. I reminded him that I didn't ask whether he was. But it was on his mind constantly. I've never met anyone who resisted the conclusion that he was gay as much as Kevin.

By the time Kevin was 18, he tried to disprove his approaching conclusion by sexually acting out with girls. He would do push-ups continually, talk about horses, and dress up as a cowboy, as if to prove he was a man, fearing that comments and accusations made by friends and onlookers might be true. He later told me that the reason he got married was to prove to himself that he wasn't gay. He said that he really loved his wife until one day, in a fit of rage, she called him a fag, and he knew that this relationship, just like most of his others, was doomed to become a place of torment rather than rest. Years ago, he told me that he thought that his dog and I were just about the only two who really loved him for who he was. We laughed when he said that he wished people could love him like his dog does. We laughed to hide our tears.

I hear from Kevin occasionally. He calls every six months or so just to check in and give us a chance to catch up on each other's lives. A few years ago, I asked him, "How's my gay friend in Tennessee doing?"

His response was a little startling. He quickly and sternly answered, "You think I chose this? I wouldn't wish this lifestyle on anyone. But I can tell you one thing. I've found people who love me and care for me. I'm not ridiculed, and I finally have some rest in my life." Kevin asked me a question the last time we talked: "Mark, do you think that God still thinks of me?"

My response? "In a good way, Kevin...in a good way."

A few months ago, I received a desperate phone call from a man who had snatched his daughter out of an unhealthy relationship with another girl, put her in his car, and just started to drive. He called me in a desperate mess, needing direction, wanting some hope, and trying to find someone to come alongside him and his wife as they wrestled through an unforeseeable and unfathomable situation with a daughter they love dearly.

Not really knowing this man, but knowing that he was hundreds of miles from home and a million miles from where he wanted to be, I said, "You come, and I'll help in any way I can."

One of our staff guys asked me, "What are you going to do when he gets here?"

I answered, "I have no idea." The issue wasn't what was going to happen; the issue was that there would be a place to go.

Jesus said, "Come to me, all you who are weary and burdened, and I will give you rest. Take my yoke upon you and learn from me, for I am gentle and humble in heart, and you will find rest for your souls. For my yoke is easy and my burden is light" (Matthew 11:28-30).

Kevin, like this man who called me, was looking for a place of rest, a place that beckons to the weary and the burdened. Kevin was definitely both. He was burdened with issues that would break the back of the world's strongest man, and weary to the point that life wasn't much worth living. Kevin was not a low-maintenance sinner. His struggles were not the fun struggles to work through. And this is what truly burdened people look like. Their baggage is a mess. It's not fun. And most people try to avoid situations where struggle is present, because the situation will wear you out if it's not resolved.

When all those around Kevin failed him, he came to Christ looking for help, relief, and compassion, trusting in His gentleness and humility. And because of the way he was treated by so many in his life who should have loved him the best, including those at his church, he defaulted to the gay lifestyle, where he found the rest he longed for and relationships that would offer, at the very least, a place to feel at home.

Sadly, because of the way Kevin was treated by so many, I doubt he will ever again darken the doors of the church, which is called to carry out Jesus' ministry to people who are hurting and in search of hope, love, and compassion.

The lesson for me was simple yet difficult to learn. Kevin exposed my own sin. My sin was a sin of judgment. I hated the sin, but I also found that I wasn't too excited about loving the sinners whom I labeled worse than me. So I avoided them, developing qualifications that people had to meet to gain my attention and help, thus eliminating the very ones God wanted to touch. My sin of selectivity was wrong. My sin of arrogance, thinking that I was better that those who struggled, was prideful and as filthy as rags. My focus was wrong as I relied on what I saw rather than what Christ saw in every person who struggles: a heart full of the possibility that it can be touched by a God who beckons all to come...without qualifications.

Parents across the country are faced every day with the challenge of having children who are living out choices that are far different from what the parents desired for them. The children don't want to change, and regardless of how much Scripture is quoted, they are determined to continue along their chosen path. To embrace an alternative lifestyle is difficult, yet to write off a relationship is a violation of what God would desire from us. I'm not just talking about a child who has chosen a gay lifestyle. I'm talking about how to love a son having an affair, a child who has committed a crime and is serving time, a daughter caught in a same-sex relationship, or a teen battling drug addiction where you're in the thick of a war, battling for his life. I'm also talking about a teen who is an embarrassment to you, a daughter whose choices always seem to be the opposite of what you hoped for her, a son who is so disrespectful, rebellious, and stubborn that he is hard to be around, or a daughter whose mouth is vicious, critical, and venomous.

God calls us to love our children in the midst of their sin so that someone is there to speak the truth to them. That way, should they choose or long for something different in their life, there is a path back to Him, an open door that offers a place of rest when they are ready to come to Him and come home.

I know what Scripture says about the way Kevin was living. And I know the choices that Kevin was making were wrong. What I originally didn't know was how to love him in the midst of his choices whether I agreed with them or not. Now I believe that God has called me to be a part of Kevin's life, not to be a judge and jury, but to offer a relationship that would counter the damage done over the years and to offer a glimpse of something that can ultimately only be found in God.

These are tough situations. A few years ago, Kevin's dad called and told me that he hasn't talked to Kevin in eight years. He said that it was hard for him to look his son in the face without thinking about what he does behind closed doors. I told him, "Then you need to quit thinking about those things. You're letting the sin be the focus and not your son."

Kevin taught me more about loving sinners. This Scripture can help all parents who disagree with the lifestyle their child has chosen: "Finally, brothers, whatever is true, whatever is noble, whatever is right, whatever is pure, whatever is lovely, whatever is admirable—if anything is excellent or praiseworthy—think about such things" (Philippians 4:8).

In the midst of thinking about what is admirable, lovely, and pure about my daughter or son, many would ask, "Where is the hope?" The hope is found in God, "being confident of this, that he who began a good work in you will carry it on to completion until the day of Christ Jesus" (Philippians 1:6). God has not finished! He will continue the work He started in our children and the work He has done through us. The challenge for parents is to make sure we don't get in His way.

Yes, set boundaries. Yes, stop enabling your child. Yes, know what you believe and where you stand. But don't eliminate or reject the one whom God has placed in your life for a reason. Loving the sinner was harder than I thought. But every sinner is someone's child...maybe yours.

Chapter 16

Not Rebellious, Just Different

■ ■ ■ ■

Sam's inappropriate behavior was unpredictable; you never knew when another incident would occur. On the flip side, another part of Sam's demeanor was predictable. Whenever he was caught doing something wrong, he was always sorrowful, tearful, apologetic, and quick to admit fault and seek forgiveness. Fifteen minutes later, the cycle began again. If he wasn't antagonizing other kids who lived with us, he was figuring out a way to disrupt conversations or interactions between people. If he could find a way around something, he would—just to prove he could beat the system. If your character had a flaw, he would detect it, needle it to death, and wear you out at your weakest point. He'd argue for argument's sake, yell just to prove that he was somebody, and thrive on negative attention, which was about the only type he could get. The odd thing about Sam is that he wasn't rebellious; he was just different.

He lived with us for a year, and the night he decided to slip away from Heartlight was the same day the foundation of our home was poured. The workers had finished late in the afternoon, and Jan and I took our two kids out to eat to celebrate the beginning of the building of our home after living two and a half years in one room as we started the Heartlight program. Our dinner that night marked the beginning of a new life for us; we were finally going to be a family of four again after a very long 30 months of living with kids. We were excited, to say the least, that in six months we were going to be able to live in our own home next to the Heartlight property.

Sam, who left Heartlight about 15 minutes after we went out for dinner, decided to stop by our new foundation first before his run through the woods and eventual return to Colorado. When he saw to our newly poured concrete, he decided to pick up a nearby sledge-hammer and break every pipe stubbed out from the foundation, ruin every copper tube that stuck out, knock down the forms that held the concrete, and slam the hammer all over the neatly finished slab, breaking off chunks of concrete.

We didn't know about the damage when we returned that night because I had spent the evening driving up and down the area high-ways looking for Sam, hoping to find him and have the millionth talk with him to calm him down and get him back on track. We didn't find him that night, but we awoke to a call from our builder, who found Sam's signature all over the new construction. He stated that he was going to have to bulldoze it all away and start over.

That's how Sam was. He was so endearing and so infuriating that I would spend hours looking in the darkness for him one night, only to want to kill him the next morning (I'm joking—sort of). What-ever he did good one moment was countered with something bad the next. People loved him and hated him almost simultaneously. He had a winsome personality that would win your heart, and a different behavior pattern that was at times so weird that we spent a lot of time scratching our heads wondering what was going to work with this young man. He baffled psychiatrists, psychologists, academic testing, counselors, and all who knew him. But he was never rebellious; he was just different.

Sarah was much the same. Growing up, this young girl didn't wear panties until age ten and didn't want people to tell her where to use the bathroom. So she "went" wherever she wanted. She grew up hateful and defiant, and she made people miserable, not because that was her intent, but because that's just the way she was. Medicine, counseling, therapy, more counseling, further treatment, and more counseling just wasn't working with this child.

When I met Sarah, she hardly spoke a word. Her mom and dad were dear people who were completely worn out, needed some relief, and begged us to help. I wanted to help this family more for the parents than I did for the girl. I saw how much they were beating themselves up, thinking they weren't good parents or had done something wrong. They thought it was all their fault. They had parented with love and logic, had (what they called) "Beaten the Kid God's Way," and had taken every parenting class offered west of the Mississippi. Nothing worked, and they came to us asking for relief and a chance to see if a different environment would work for their daughter because nothing else had.

Sarah acted as if she were eight when she came to us. A little over a year later, she left acting like the 17-year-old she was. But it was not an easy process. When she came to Heartlight, she didn't get along with anyone—staff or kids. She was obstinate, obnoxious, and selfish, and she pretty much demanded that all of us on our property center our lives around her. Our psychiatrist said she had a personality disorder. I disagreed—I was sure this girl had *no* personality. As time passed, Sarah changed. I recall the night the staff got excited because she hula-hooped in front of everyone and finally showed that she could come out of her protective shell of negativity. She continued to mature and come out of her shell, and she fell in love with our horses. Toward the end of her time with us, she was acting as normal as any other 17-year-old.

Sarah, like Sam, was just wired different from most folks. And when one is wired differently, the programming process must be reworked. She wasn't rebellious; she just interpreted others' actions as attacks on her, so she responded in kind. Reprogramming her thoughts through a steady dose of wonderful wisdom and positive relationships with peers and adults worked in the life of this young lady. She had been so bad before coming to Heartlight that when she returned home and started to rebel, her dad called and laughed with us because he finally had a normal teen—something he had dreamed of for years.

Macy was adopted from China into a family of love and warmth. Rarely do I see a family that has been as affectionate and loving to their kids as this family. Mom and Dad were genuine, the other kids were loving, and birth order was followed, but for some reason, Macy just couldn't connect with the way her new family operated. She distanced herself from her sisters. She didn't like to be touched. She enjoyed spending time by herself. This wouldn't have been a problem except for the fact that this family enjoyed doing things together. She didn't want help with homework and drove herself crazy trying to do everything on her own. She acted as if everyone was going to leave her. She often made comments that questioned others' love for her. Some said she was insecure. Others said she had attachment issues. Call it what you want. When she came to live with us, it was evident that she was just different. What was being interpreted as rebellion was really normalcy for her. What her parents thought was abnormal was really normal for her because of the way she had lived the first eight years of her life.

Sam, Sarah, and Macy all appeared to be rebellious. But the greater issue was that the problems were fueled by well-meaning parents trying to put wrong or too high-expectations on a child who wasn't wired to respond in a normal way. These kids were different. Their parents tried to enforce expectations on them, and when those expectations didn't correspond to the way the teens were wired, the teens rebelled. And these teens weren't going to change. Their parents had to learn to change their expectations for these particular children.

In each of these situations, the parents were extremely frustrated at what their teen didn't achieve, rather than pleased by the levels of interaction their teen did achieve. When we helped parents change their expectations of their unique child, they projected a new message to their child. The formerly negative differences became positive points of uniqueness.

This was a two-step process. The first step was the parents' recognition that something was different. This is hard to accept because it includes the loss of what was longed for and is now not going to happen—not in the way it was expected. Let me give you an example.

Parents who want to have a loving and affectionate relationship with a daughter may adopt a child who is incapable of fulfilling that expectation. These parents are going to feel a great sense of loss when they realize that this just isn't going to happen. For these parents to continue to place that expectation on a child who is *unable* to fulfill what is being asked of her is to ask for disaster. Parents will be disappointed, and kids will be frustrated.

I tell parents all the time to lower their expectations, which is the second step, so their child can flourish and perhaps one day make up for the unfulfilled hope. When parents expect too much from a child who is incapable of rising to the occasion and meeting that expectation, the child's frustration and parents' hurt and anger are the perfect recipe for rebellion. Love, trust, and communication are lost, and the family spirals downward out of control.

Sam, Sarah, and Macy flourished while they were with us. They flourished because we had different expectations for them. When we convinced the parents to recognize their frustrations, change their expectations, and look at their teen as different rather than rebellious, relationships changed. I personally think that the changed relationship was far better—because it was more real—than the relationship the parents had expected.

If you are resonating with this chapter and recognize your child in Sam, Sarah, or Macy, be careful not to allow your child's difference to justify disrespect, disobedience, or dishonesty. I tell people all the time that if I can train dogs and horses to be respectful, surely a teen can learn the same. In addition, this difference should never excuse teens from being responsible. They may not learn or respond in the same way that others do, but being different does not give anyone an excuse to remain immature. Parents are responsible to help a child, no matter how different, grow up.

Setting boundaries is important in this process and in any household, especially if your child thinks, behaves, and operates differently than you do. Make sure that boundaries are set, understood, and enforced.

When a parent has a child who is wired in a different configuration than others in the family, who sees things differently than the way others in the family perceive things, it is important for Mom and Dad to know these differences. If they don't, they will spend their whole lives in frustration and will destroy their relationship with their teen.

Quite honestly, different is just that—different. I don't want to blow air in your ear and tell you that if you'll adjust, everything will be fine. It doesn't work that way. In all honesty, things won't always be fine. You might spend 75 percent of your time with your child when things aren't fine, and the other 25 percent worrying about the 75 percent. Parents have a choice to make. They can either allow a child who is different to constantly drain their energy in hopes of getting something they will probably never get, or they can drop some expectations and be content with the good they do receive. It's tough. It's hard. And I'm convinced of two things: It's even harder on your teens who are living this, and God is excited that you are involved in the life of this different child. Yes, He is excited. Nothing goes unnoticed. He knows the number of hairs on your head and knows when the smallest of birds falls to the ground. Believe me, He knows.

Chapter 17

Are Bad Kids Making
My Teen Rebel?

■ ■ ■ ■

Wade's parents called me with a concern that most families have even if they never express it: how to keep their son from hanging around the "bad kids." They began to tell me about Wade, letting me know how his rebellion kicks in the minute he leaves their front door and then accelerates to a high level of fighting, yelling, and screaming when they confront his peer-influenced behavior when he returns home. Wade's parents were tired, they felt as if they couldn't control their teen, and they were ready to quit. They dejectedly shared about how great a kid their 16-year-old son is and, at the same time, how disappointed they have been with all the trouble he gets in whenever he is around his friends.

His dad told me that either the situation had to change, his son was going to have to leave, or this father was going to leave before he had a heart attack. His final question to me was this: "Why is my son being so rebellious?"

After spending a couple of hours talking further about Wade, I shared with his parents that I didn't think he was rebelling at all. Dad exploded his frustration on me and questioned how it could be anything but rebellion. He stated that Wade violated every principle they taught, every rule they set. He said Wade was irresponsible and, while always sorry for his actions, didn't show much remorse for the impact his actions had on their family.

Dad further ranted that his son was a chameleon and adapted to just about any group he was with. Dad quoted the statements he shared with Wade: "If you swim with sharks, you're gonna get bit," "bad company corrupts good morals," and "birds of a feather flock together." The problem was that Wade listened to all the comments his dad shared, but he still came home looking like a demoralized, feather-coated, shark-bitten, guilty kid who just couldn't help but be influenced by others. Dad said that if he had a nickel for every time he quoted 1 Corinthians 10:13, he would be an extremely wealthy man. Wade's family wanted to know what parents are to do about all these bad kids their kids are hanging around.

Good question, but let me set the stage a little first.

Teens like to "hang out," "chill," or "do nothing." As long as they are with peers, friends, or just others who look like them, they enjoy being together. They move in herds, form alliances, and love to belong. Because of this deep desire, they want to spend time together. Do you think hanging out at Starbucks is about the coffee or being with friends? Do you think going to the mall is more about being seen and socialization or about shopping? Do you think all the texting they do is about the transfer of information or just wanting to be connected? It's a given; they are going to spend time with others.

The people your teen hangs out with will be either more exposed to the world or less exposed. The chance that they've all had equal exposure is about one in a million. So when these teens get together, they're going to talk, share true stories, and make up other stories. And somebody's eyes are going to be opened (the teens with less exposure—probably the "good" Christian teens). They do it for identity, excitement, curiosity, or maybe just because there's nothing else to do or they're bored. They want to connect with one another because even though there is quite a bit of communication, there is very little true connection or intimacy (and I don't mean the physical kind) happening in their peer relationships.

They may hang out with the people they do because they feel comfortable with them and identify with others who are struggling more than they identify with the "good kids" who seem to have it all together.

So here are some questions for you. What is your teen finding in others that she is not finding at home? Why is your son identifying with these bad kids instead of other good kids? What is it that your teen likes about the unchurched, the skaters, the surfers, or other groups that you might not care for? These are important questions because your child might be showing his hand through her attachment with these "bad kids." I encourage you to show more concern about your teen's drive to attach to these others than about the other kids themselves.

The issue of bad kids may have more to do with the "influencee" than it does the "influencer." There will always be someone out there who can influence your child in a negative way. You will never get away from that regardless of where you move or what limits you put around who your teen hangs out with. There is always someone out there you don't have any control over. So your emphasis should be on your own child, not those other kids whom you will never eliminate or control. Usually, those kids who are negative influences on your teen are those who influence your teen to do something, be something, or say something that you don't want him to. As your child gets older, you'll find that peer influence becomes greater and your influence diminishes.

Wanting to hold on to your child's innocence in his early years is normal. You don't want him to "know things" yet. You want him to enjoy life and enjoy childhood as long as he can. But this culture of adolescence has changed, and many teens are being exposed to the world at a much earlier age than those who grew up 20 years ago. The overabundance of information, the loose speech, and the societal acceptance of what simply wasn't accepted before place an extreme pressure on parents to teach their children about the real world they are entering *before* children find out about that world through friends who have already been exposed. My point is simple: We must train our teens to fight before they go into battle. This is much better than cleaning up the mess of a child who was ill-prepared and got shot down (or shot others) on the battlefront.

If your teen is under the age of 16, you must limit exposure and control the areas of his life where he has not yet developed the internal control mechanisms of good choices, wise decisions, and healthy behaviors. These internal controls develop as parents allow a child to make choices and decisions at a rate that will prepare him for the time he turns 16 so he can function adequately in the world.

Why 16? Because the minute you drop a set of car keys in the hands of your teen, his world and yours changes. That is the time when you must be able to trust that you have trained him and can turn him loose to make wise decisions and good choices. You must now trust God more than ever before to watch over him and protect him should he get in harm's way. That's why your relationship with those "bad kids" now changes as well. They are now influences to be reckoned with, and you can't easily keep your teen away from them.

Wade's parents finally figured out that they had not really trained their son in the areas where he was falling down. They didn't accept responsibility for Wade's inappropriate behavior, nor did they excuse it away, but they realized they had some catching up to do. Wade's parents never thought that Wade would drink alcohol, so they never talked about it. They also thought that because they had told him he needed to be a gentleman and treat girls like ladies, he would never become sexually involved with his girlfriend. So they never talked about sex when he started dating. They never thought he'd quit the football team, want to stop going to church, or decline to go to summer camp. Because they never thought about these things, they never talked about them. So when Wade started to be influenced by others and these things started to happen, Wade's parents found themselves having to clean up a few messes.

And there are teens that your teen doesn't need to hang around. I would encourage you to make sure that your teen, as a rule, doesn't hang around kids you don't know and who are already out of high school unless they are Christian youth workers. Older kids aren't bad, but they have been exposed to more, and you might want to keep that exposure in check for as long as you can. Another rule of thumb for your daughter might be not to let her date anyone outside of her school setting, or anyone who is more than two years older than she is. Simple boundaries like these might help prevent battles.

If your teen gets into trouble with a friend, let that other teen know you want to meet with him before your teen gets to hang out with him again. Let him know of your displeasure with what happened and how disappointed you are with your son or daughter and with him. Wouldn't it be easier to have this type of conversation with someone you know and have a relationship with? Surely God places people in our lives for a reason. He may be placing a "bad kid" in your child's life for a reason. Instead of automatically eliminating the friend who causes conflict, consider that there is a bigger issue than just keeping your teen from being negatively influenced. Conflict is a precursor to change, and this conflict caused by your teen's inappropriate behavior, perhaps influenced by another teen, might just be that precursor to a change that your child needs to make.

If your teen *is* that "bad kid" the other parents don't want their kids hanging out with, I would encourage you to make sure to have discussions, set rules, enforce consequences, and don't enable your teen to continue the "bad boy" or "bad girl" habits. Let me assure you here—I've never met a bad kid. I've met some who have participated in bad behavior, who maybe bought the beer instead of just drinking it, or someone who came up with the bad idea that everyone else followed. But truly bad? No. One is a leader; one is a follower. One is an idea person, the other is bored. One is stupid in coming up with an idea, the other is stupid for following it. It's all in the way you view it. One parent may look at a "bad kid" as one who influences a child negatively. Another would view the same "bad kid" as an opportunity to be positively influenced. So if you have a "bad kid," don't abandon your teen; your teen needs you desperately. If everyone else is running from your child, you be the one to run to him.

No, I've truly never met a bad kid. Have you?

Chapter 18

Parents Adopting Kids and Kids Adopting Parents

■ ■ ■ ■

never used to understand my wife, Jan, when she would tell me that one of the greatest losses in her life was not graduating from college with a nursing degree, fulfilling a childhood dream that would have enabled her to serve God in the way she thought He wanted to use her. Whenever she would bring this up, I found myself getting a little mad that she could even think that way. I remember many times saying to her, "Now wait a minute—you had to drop out of college because we were pregnant. Are you saying you didn't want to have our daughter?"

She'd always tell me, "That's not what I'm saying." My usual response was, "I just don't understand why you would rather have a college degree than have your daughter." This conversation would trail off into nowhere. She would be upset that I was missing the point, and I would be still a little mad at her because she couldn't appreciate what she had in our daughter. I thought she wasn't being grateful for what God had chosen for us; she thought she had missed an opportunity. I wondered why she couldn't be happy for what she has; she wondered what it would have been like to fulfill the longing she had had for so many years. I told her she came out ahead; she told me she felt a loss. I told her she should be able to let go of what she didn't have; she told me it was hard to let go of a dream. I told her God has a plan; she told me He *had* a plan. I told her it was no big deal; she told me it *was* a big deal. I told her she wasn't hearing what I was saying; she told me I wasn't hearing what she was saying. I agreed. She agreed that I agreed. And let me assure you that these comments weren't always said with loving smiles on our faces.

Then one day, I got it. I realized that because I never want to be wrong and because I always want to provide the very best for my wife, I bulldozed my way right past some of her heart's longings and desires. I just kept plowing the field of God's plan for our life without even knowing that I was covering up a hole in her heart that first needed to heal. I realized that I had ignored some very real and very deep parts of my wife's life. I missed the heart of what she was saying and attempted to prove her wrong to justify that everything I had done was right.

I also I realized that in my pursuit of being the perfect husband, I was covering my own losses in life in order to create a perfect home that housed perfect people. When Jan felt a loss, especially one that happened during our marriage, I felt as if that meant I had done something wrong—or hadn't done something I should have. Her loss of a dream triggered in me a feeling of inadequacy. After all, how could a perfect husband miss a huge hole like that in his wife's life? He couldn't.

I finally came to realize that I wasn't the perfect husband. When I let that curtain of perfection have its final call, I saw where I had missed many people in the course of pursuing my own dream of perfection. And a mind-set of perfection not only gives the perfectionist the delusion that everything he is doing is right but also keeps him from seeing what might be wrong in others. He misses the opportunity to recognize hurt, harm, struggle, difficulty, and broken hearts in the midst of his own family.

I needed Jan not to feel loss, not to be depressed, and not to tell me where she was not complete. I needed her to be okay, to be something she wasn't. I needed it because it fed the image that I was trying desperately to sustain—an image that life was good, everything was okay, and God is great. How selfish I was (probably still am). I couldn't see that I had my eyes constantly focused on me!

You may be asking yourself how this all fits into the topic of parents adopting kids and kids adopting their new stepparents. I think it fits perfectly. Here's why: Adopting is a wonderful experience, and bringing a stepmom or a stepdad into a family to create a new opportunity for a broken family is a wonderful thing. *But regardless of how good things are, they don't always undo the losses that have occurred in someone's life.* To ignore those losses and not deal with them only postpones the healing until another event, such as going off to college, getting married, having children, or experiencing a death in the family.

The Adopted Child

Most people get pretty excited when they see someone adopt an older child. In all the excitement and joy, many forget about the losses this child has experienced. Some parents rightly put all the bad images and experiences these children have accumulated in their little hearts on the back burner so their focus can be on all that is good as they bring the new life into their family. But when a family ignores a child's losses, or when a family believes its nurture can overcome the natural damage done in the past, the possibility of turmoil in the adolescent years increases. Damage will rise to the surface as a child moves from the concrete thinking of preadolescence into the abstract thinking of adolescence.

As young hearts begin to move into the new world of adolescence, a number of shifts take place. They begin to think differently. Instead of just acknowledging that a battleship floats, they begin to ask why a battleship floats. Rather than accepting traditions and habits as the way things have always been, they question why their family holds to these traditions and habits. They question, search, observe, think, and contemplate in ways they never have before. They wonder about things that never piqued their interest earlier. They begin to have feelings they've never had. Some might have new questions about God that sound like denial of His existence, but they may really be assimilating Him into deeper areas of their life. They become aware of the opposite sex, the darkness of the world, and the imperfections of their mom and dad. They begin the process of solidifying their own identity and figuring out their place in the world. To an adopted child, especially one from a foreign country, this all becomes a pretty big deal.

The adopted child wonders what would have happened if she had not been adopted. She might think about what her birth mother was like and why she abandoned her. The adopted child might wonder what she lost by leaving her original country. If she was older when she was adopted, the hurt of abandonment, time in an orphanage, or just that fact that she didn't have what she should have had may have caused some damage in her life. She might express a desire to one day meet her birth mother (a desire that is more about finding out who she is than a reflection of her love for that birth mother). Internationally adopted kids wonder about their old language. They think about the difference in their looks and maybe in their accent. They might feel out of place and out of touch with their roots. They might fantasize about what it would have been like not to have been adopted, especially if there is currently conflict and hardship in the family. It's a time of questioning, as it is for every other young teen entering adolescence. But the adopted child's life began a little differently, and she has experienced many things that others her age have not.

One parent I know didn't want her adopted son from the Ukraine to have any more losses in his life. She told him when he came to her family that old things have passed away, and now all things are new. This statement was an affirmation of his new life, new family, and new path. And the strategy worked for a while. But then Alex began thinking at different levels, and he thought about when his mother had died. He remembered when he went to live with his aunt and when she died. He began to think about the abuse he experienced in the orphanage. He had only one picture of him with his father, and Alex knew nothing else about him. Alex wondered where his two brothers were. His parents' response to Alex's thoughts were that "old things have passed away." But they really hadn't, and Alex's subsequent rebellion was an effort to get someone to acknowledge the hurts in his life and help him to heal.

If parents take the path I did when my wife started sharing her losses with me, they'll miss the true heart of their child, and their teen may move from temporary confusion to a long-term conflict and rebellion. My encouragement to families is not to respond to their child in the way that I responded to my wife, but to work hard to see the loss from their child's perspective.

Here's what I have learned that might apply to teens wrestling with issues of loss in their lives:

Loss Happens, and That's Okay

First of all, it's okay to have loss in your own life, and it's okay for your loved ones to have loss in theirs. Loss happens. No one gets through life without it. Life is hard, people are cruel, we all fall short, and our need for a Savior accentuates the true condition of life. It's tough. So to ignore the fact that loss exists in people's lives is to ignore the heart of the person who has experienced it.

Does loss look any different in the life of an adopted teen? Yes. But it's not because one person's loss is any bigger or more dramatic than any other person's. It is because of parents' response when their adopted teen experiences the normal questioning of her identity. Parents of adopted kids sometimes ignore the questioning of identity because they have worked so hard to give them a new, healthy identity. I have seen the goodness of parents who sacrificially give a wonderful new life to their adopted child. And so many times I see parents live in denial that their child could be experiencing deep loss. I know what I'm talking about. More than one-third of the kids who have lived with us at Heartlight were adopted. We spend more time helping parents understand the losses their teens have experienced than we spend helping teens work through and get on the other side of their losses.

It's okay to have losses. It's all right not to have it all together. It's fine not to be perfect. And it's acceptable not to have all the answers. If you acknowledge these things to your child, it might give her affirmation when she is wrestling through a multitude of questions. You might help her not to deny the presence of good or the presence of

God, but rather to seek the presence of both in a way that helps her through this tough stage of adolescence.

Loss in your teen's life is not a reflection on the quality of the job you have done as a parent. I often hear parents make comments like these:

- "How can you feel this way after all we've done for you?"

- "We rescued you from a life that was a mess; why would you want to go back there?"

- "What do you mean you're unhappy? We've sacrificed everything for you."

- "How can you question our love for you? We sought you out."

- "How could something that started out so good end up so bad?"

- "What do you mean you don't feel a part of our family? What have we not done for you?"

- "We've treated you as one of our own; how can you feel the way you do?"

- "Why would you want to meet your birth mother? She gave you up long ago."

These are just like the comments I made to Jan when she started to share about the loss she felt in her life. I believed her losses were a reflection of my performance as a husband. Jan and I met with a counselor for a year and a half to get some help dealing with the losses in our lives. I remember our counselor looking at me when I shared how Jan's losses made me feel irresponsible and inadequate as a husband. She pointedly said, without batting an eye, "Who died and made you God?" She didn't follow up the statement with a comment. She just let that question hang there for a moment, just long enough for me to realize that I was trying to be more like God to my wife than like a husband to her. Our counselor's comments reminded me that my wife needed a husband; she already had God.

Jan needed what adopted kids need: someone to stand next to them in their losses, not someone who denies those losses. They need someone to comfort them in the midst of their hurts and questions, not someone to convince them their feelings are wrong. They need someone who will tell them it's okay not to have it all together, not someone who tries to explain everything away, give a good excuse, make them feel better, or question the existence of their pain.

My wife's losses in life were not about me. But whether I allowed them to be real in her life was certainly about me. When I tried to keep the losses from surfacing in her life, I also kept the sweet grace of Jesus from filling up those holes in her life and healing her heart in ways that my denial would never do.

The same is true for you and your adopted teen.

The Adopted Stepparent

Stepparenting is one of the toughest roles an adult will ever step into. It may be easy when the stepkids are young, but something about the onset of adolescence can bring out a whole different side of a stepchild who is rethinking things in her life. A wonderful stepparent who came into a family's life and filled holes left by divorce or death can appear to be a horse of a different color when stepkids enter the adolescent years. It's not because the stepparent has changed. It is because this budding teen is beginning to view life through a somewhat different lens.

Adoption is a special act of love that happens at a crucial time in the life of a family and begins a grafting process that deepens relationships and connections as time passes. Whether two parents adopt a new child into their family or a child "adopts" a new stepparent, conflicts can eventually arise as family members recognize the losses they have experienced. But these conflicts can actually strengthen the new family's bonds. The presence of struggle in any relationship does not always denote the separating of two people or the deterioration of a relationship. Conflict can actually bond them closer together. The adoption of a stepparent into a family may create an environment where losses rise to the surface and show themselves in the behaviors of a teen. Children who are not yet teens can usually welcome a stepparent into a family. They feel as if the family is now a family again. There's a mom and a dad, single parenting is gone, and another chapter in life has begun. But when kids in the family "turn teen," their thinking pattern can match that of teens who have been adopted. They go through some of the same reflection, contemplation, and introspection. These new adolescents begin to look at what they have and what they don't have. In the midst of taking this inventory, they pay special attention to those "thought triggers" that remind them of where they come up short, how they feel inadequate, what they wish were different, or how they have experienced loss. Sadly, the presence of something good might remind them of something that wasn't so good. And the better that good thing is, the more painful the loss may feel. Here are some examples.

A stepdad's presence in the home might remind teens of what they don't have anymore if they've lost their dad's daily presence to death or divorce. A new stepmom might remind teens of when they lost their mother or of a painful time when they were with their mother. Some teens feel that accepting a stepparent constitutes a rejection of their parent, or it may make them feel disloyal to the now absent parent. Usually, the better the stepparent is, the harder the loss is to take. A good stepparent might remind a teen of all that has been lost.

When a teen becomes disrespectful to the stepparent and emotions begin to flair, it is so, so important for the stepparent to realize that their teen's new realizations are short-term and will usually pass as long as the parent and stepparent don't overreact and push a child into rebellion. That rebellion could be justified in the mind of the teen and move him to believe that he is defending the legend, loyalty, and love of an absent parent. It's a mind-set that says, "I'll stick up for you, Mom," or, "Don't worry, Dad. I'll never forget you," and many teens will fight to the death under those circumstances.

No loss or feeling of loss ever justifies a teen being disrespectful, disobedient, dishonest, hateful, evil, apathetic, contemptuous, or nasty to a stepparent. So I encourage parents to enter this conflict with a great sense of understanding and with a great deal of strength. Make sure you put your spiritual armor on! Understanding is rooted in accepting your child's losses and committing to allow him to struggle through his feelings and wrestle with the areas of loss and prior damage.

Create a family atmosphere where struggles are allowed, but control the behavior in areas where your child cannot control it. Clearly communicate rules based on established family beliefs. Immaturity displayed through poor choices and foolish decisions demands boundaries and limitations. Defiance demands consequences—not to be punitive, but as correction—to let her know she can't hurt others intentionally just because she hurts. Let your teen know that it's okay to struggle, but it's not okay to be disrespectful. It's okay not to have it together, but it's not okay to engage in dangerous behavior to fill the voids that her losses have created. It's all right to have bad days, but it's not all right to cause others to have bad days. Your job is to show your child how to struggle well—not to try to alleviate all struggles or gloss over them, but to walk straight through them with faith, hope, love, and grace.

As a parent or stepparent, you have to remember not to take her behavior or rejection personally. You're not the problem. Some of the young girls who live with us have sabotaged a good time together riding horses, waterskiing, or just sitting around talking with comments that made me scratch my head and wonder if I did something wrong. I didn't. But my good actions toward them and their enjoyment of those times reminds them of what they don't have with their parents. I can correct them and hand out a consequence for their disrespect or selfishness, but sometimes a better strategy is to learn when to let some things go—to just drop it and let it pass. Sometimes it is better to leave well enough alone because your correction will not actually correct what is happening. And just as a fool appears wise when he keeps his mouth shut, a good stepparent learns when to say something and when to let it go. Does it hurt? Oh yeah, but welcome to parenting. If parents begin to respond every time they are hurt by their teen, everyone will be miserable.

Don't play into teens' strategy to have you pay for what they lost. They must recognize that loss and work through it. And they will. Given time and stepparents who ensure that their struggling teens maintain responsibility for their feelings, teens will get through their losses. And you want them to because if they don't, they'll fill those voids with unhealthy activities that will only create further trauma and loss.

As I said earlier, a stepparent's position in the family is a tough role to fill. I tell those who choose this role to walk softly and carry a big stick—in that order. Walk softly toward your new stepchild. Learn to walk softly away to calm issues that you have no part of. Learn to walk softly in front of your stepchild to prepare a safe path for her to walk. Walk softly behind your stepchild to ensure she's moving in the right direction. And walk softly with her to let her know of your willingness to help her through anything that might arise because of your involvement in her life. What about the big stick? Pray that you won't have to pull that out often because of the soft way that you walk. Many people try to use the stick first. Use it only as backup—seldom used and seldom seen. Let your walk be your talk.

Chapter 19

The Visible Expression of Invisible Issues

■ ■ ■ ■

Katy was rebelling against her parents. There was no doubt in anyone's mind about that. She was defiant and wouldn't listen. She walked out the front door in the middle of her mother's conversations with her, and she didn't say a word during any meal the family ate together. She was successful in school, respectful of teachers, and cordial to everyone else. But the minute she got home, her demeanor and her behavior changed. She began to tell her parents what she was doing instead of asking for their permission. She came home when she wanted to, disregarding curfew and any threats of consequences for staying out late.

Katy had everything taken away from her, but she didn't care because she knew she was making life difficult for her parents. Her plan was working. She was determined to teach her parents a lesson. She was on a mission to make her parents pay because they wouldn't pay attention to anything she was saying. After I met Katy and spent some time talking with her, I came to the conclusion that the one who is rebelling the most is sometimes actually the healthiest member of the family, the one who perceives the truth of the family's circumstance when everyone else is living in denial. In Katy's situation, this seemed to be accurate.

In the mid-1960s, our family visited my aunt and uncle in McLean, Virginia. I was a ten-year-old boy eager to see Washington DC and all the sites I had read about in my *Weekly Reader*. I visited the Washington Monument, the Lincoln Memorial, the Jefferson Memorial, the Iwo Jima Memorial, and George Washington's home, Mount Vernon. I spent a couple of days at the Smithsonian Institute and visited the Tomb of the Unknown Soldier and the gravesite of John F. Kennedy. I went to the Capitol and walked through the building with my jaw dropped, eyes wide open, and ears tuned to our guide's description of every detail of this wonderful structure.

But those aren't the things I remember the most today about the whole trip. It was the drinking fountains. There were always two drinking fountains right next to each other throughout Washington. And each one had a little two-inch sign over the stainless steel basin where people would come for a refreshing drink of water. I was chided by a guide who informed me that I was drinking out of the wrong water fountain. I was supposed to drink out of the one that said "For Whites Only" and not the one that stated "For Coloreds Only." The same thing happened when I walked into the wrong bathroom.

As we walked outside and began our stroll down the Washington Mall to get a bite to eat, we passed hundreds of black people who were marching around the Washington Mall with signs and placards and chanting. Policemen were everywhere, and two white policemen were yelling at two black women, encouraging them to do something— perhaps change their color, go home, or quit griping. I asked my dad what the policemen were doing, and he said to keep walking. That night as we were eating around my aunt and uncle's dining room table, I asked about the water fountains. It was a short discussion. My dad continued to eat as if he didn't hear me. I put two and two together. The two-inch signs over the stainless steel basins, the two policemen "encouraging" the two black ladies, and my father's silence all brought about a realization to this ten-year-old boy. I realized that the one who was rebelling might be the healthiest of the whole bunch.

Katy's problem started when she was 15 and began the normal adolescent reflection process. She began to think about all the years when she had taken showers with her father—right up until she was 12 years old. She brought up the subject in a very gentle way at the dinner table one night and asked a question that I get asked often. She asked her mother when she thought it was inappropriate for a dad to be taking showers with his daughter. Katy told me that you would have thought she had just told the family she had murdered someone.

Quietness descended, mouths filled with food, and Katy's mother nervously stumbled for words as her heart raced and her voice cracked. Her mother said, "I think when the daughter can tell the difference."

It was a simple answer that now opened the door for a follow-up question. Katy asked, "When do you think that age is, Mom?" Katy shared the story with me with a sense of pride and enthusiasm, just like a lawyer winning a court case.

Her mother answered, "About two years old." Katy's next question changed her family forever. "Then why did you let Dad take showers with me until I was twelve?"

Katy said her two brothers suddenly left the dinner table, Mom didn't answer, and Dad just continued eating like nothing was being said. Sometimes the healthiest of the whole bunch might be the one who is rebelling.

A teen's actions may be the only visible expression that something isn't right. The outward expression could be the only indicator of the inward conflict that a family is experiencing and has not yet committed to change. To assume that a teen's inappropriate behavior is the teen's problem—to the exclusion of other possibilities—eliminates the consideration that the problem may have been generated not by the culture she is living in or the poor choices she is making, but from within the family. Something was terribly wrong within Katy's family, and they needed to attend to the damage her father's poor choices caused and to their inability or unwillingness to stop something that became inappropriate. Katy's father was being helpful when she was two years old. His actions moved into the realm of sexual abuse when they continued into her junior high years.

Katy's questions were appropriate. They began a much-needed process of bringing hidden issues to the surface. Her family's non-response spiraled Katy into true rebellion. She was rebelling against something that was unquestionably wrong. When her first approach didn't work, she resorted to one that was more severe. Her rebellion got a better response from her family than her simple questions did. This chapter is not about sexual abuse. When a normal teen faces anything he thinks is wrong and his family members cannot or will not see it, he may very well rebel as another means of getting the issue some attention. Here are other circumstances I have seen that moved a teen into rebellion when the family covered them up.

Amanda's grandfather visited once a month and inappropriately French kissed his nine, ten, and twelve-year-old granddaughters, but no one said anything because this patriarch of the family was held in high regard in society. No one wanted to rock the boat.

Lea had a 25-year-old brother who came home drunk every Saturday night but got up every Sunday morning to teach an eighth-grade Sunday school class. Everyone acted on Sunday morning as if nothing happened the night before.

Caleb finally decided to stand up against his dad, the pastor of a church, who treated his wife (Caleb's mother) with disrespect and disdain. He ignored Caleb's requests that he treat his wife with respect, forcing Caleb to move from asking to demanding. When that didn't work, he resorted to physical aggression. His mother didn't say a word when the dad had Caleb arrested for punching him.

Danielle's mother keeps bringing men to the house in hopes of finding someone who has money. Danielle feels uncomfortable whenever she is at home by herself or with her friends. Her requests for her mom to stop are ignored.

Joshua's dad gambled away the kids' college funds and racked up debt up to his eyeballs, but everyone kept acting as if nothing was happening. Joshua said it was like being on a slowly sinking boat. Items were repossessed, creditors were calling and harassing, and the cable service was turned off. When Josh tried to talk to his mother about what was going on, she told him to mind his own business.

Uncle Sean loved to come visit his brother's family. Like clockwork, in the middle of the night, Uncle Sean would sneak into Beth's room, take off his clothes, and have sex with Beth, saying that if she ever told anyone, he would destroy her reputation. Beth was scared to death and remained silent, fearing in shame that her uncle would talk about the times her body responded to his advances. She was also afraid of destroying the family that she loved dearly. She drank heavily on weekends when he came to visit.

Nathan's mom would "hit the sauce" a little too much every night when she came home, verbally abuse everyone in the family, and fall asleep on the couch. Nathan's dad would put her to bed, and the cycle began again the next morning. No one talked about the elephant in Nathan's house, so when he brought up his mom's alcohol abuse, his dad told him that his mother was just tired.

Crystal's 24-year-old brother didn't have a job, played video games all day, smoked dope in his room, and stayed up all night. The family acted as if this was normal behavior. He was a mess, and Crystal was embarrassed to invite friends to their house. When she questioned her mom about what was going on, Mom's response was that it was his house too.

Travis's dad constantly made sexual comments about Travis's girl-friend when she was present and when she was absent. The dad ignored Travis's request for him to stop. So when Dad tried to tell Travis what to do, he paid him right back by ignoring him. Until people started listening to Travis, Travis felt justified in not listening to them.

I could go on and on with other examples, but these demonstrate that some situations deteriorate so far that rebellion is the only way teens can instigate change. Katy's mom wasn't just hesitant to say anything; she was scared to say anything. She later told me she knew that what her husband was doing was wrong and hoped that he and Katy would just grow out of it, and that Katy would forget that it ever happened. When Katy brought up the situation at the dinner table, mom said that she was surprised, embarrassed, and relieved all at the same time. She tried to explain to Katy that she was afraid that if she stood up against her husband, he would leave her. Katy explained to her that she understood her reasoning but felt abandoned by a mother who was supposed to protect her. Katy's older brothers also abandoned her. When she confronted them, they said they thought the shower incidents were always a little weird but stayed out of it because Dad would punish them if they spoke up. They said they figured that if it needed to stop, Mom would have said something. They also admitted that it was the first thing that came to their minds when their dad suggested their family adopt a little Russian girl. Katy's mother and brothers abandoned her, and her dad ignored her. Probably the greatest damage to Katy came from her father, who acted as if her question wasn't even worth answering. I wonder which is worse, the act of abuse or the lack of resolution, closure, or restoration after abuse has occurred.

Feeling lost and alone, with two years of high school left before she could leave home, Katy felt that the best thing she could do was to stand up for what was right. Because her family would not accept any responsibility for what they had all done or not done, she let them all know how damaged she had been. She chose to do whatever she wanted, so she was labeled rebellious. And rebellious she was—in a good way.

If you're a youth minister or a teacher trying to figure out why a good kid you know is struggling so much at home, I encourage you to look beyond the behaviors that parents tell you about. Something may be lurking in the closet that needs to be brought to the light. And it may not be in the child's closet, but in the family closet. And even though a kid appears to be "perfect" in youth group, class, Sunday school, or social activities, don't assume that all is well back on the Ponderosa. I can't tell you the number of times people have started a conversation with me with the words "I've never told anybody this." You may be a teen's only lifeline, so toss that buoy carefully and pull her in to a place of safety so she doesn't drown in her rebellious thrashings.

If you're a parent who sees something happening within your family that you know is wrong, today is the day to expose it. Every day that it goes unexposed is one more day it can damage your child's life and yours. Exposing what's already there doesn't make anything worse, it just brings to the surface what's already happening so you can deal with it. I wasn't any worse the day I was told I had skin cancer. I already had it, but now I knew it and could do something to correct it. When I confront men about wrong behaviors, moms about their bad habits, or brothers and uncles about their inappropriate actions, they feel a sense of relief, even in their anger, shame, and embarrassment. It is the fulfillment of John 8:32, "The truth shall set you free," and the beginning of a process that moves to healing.

Once healthy changes are made within a family, a teen's rebellious behavior often ceases. It ceases because the point has been made, healthy relationships can now be formed, and the recognition of wrongdoing brings about healing and restoration. The process isn't easy, but it's good. As I said earlier, sometimes the one who is rebelling is the healthiest one in the whole bunch.

I have the honor to serve on the board of directors for America World Adoption, located in McLean, Virginia. I have many opportunities to travel to Washington DC and walk through government buildings. Every time I get a drink of water, I chuckle and thank the Lord for those who rebelled and brought about a healthier atmosphere for us all.

Chapter 20

We'll Keep the Light On for You

■ ■ ■ ■

've spent a lot of pages telling you all the ways that rebellion usually isn't really rebellion. But what if you are convinced that's what you have on your hands? If you've searched and searched, looking for answers as to why your teen is acting the way he is, and you're still wondering, *What's happening to my teen?* you might have a teen that is displaying a dose of good ol' teen rebellion. But even that isn't always a bad thing. When a teen bucks the system, shows displeasure about parts of life, and wants independence, he may have some good longings and desires that he is acting out inappropriately. The key for you is to guide these usually short-lived escapades of experimentation into opportunities to help your teen grow up, accept responsibility for his life, and apply some good lessons you taught him in his younger years.

I've seen hundreds and hundreds and hundreds of teen lives. And you can believe me when I tell you that what you have taught your teen has not been a waste. The seeds you have sown in his life will come to fruition, just as the Bible has promised. None of the good things you have done will come back void. The great lessons your teen learned from you in his earlier years will bring him back in due time.

It's the "due time" part that's the kicker.

We don't know when that time is. It may be a month, or it may be 20 years. However long it takes, I can assure you that your posture during this dark time will affect the amount of time your child spends wandering aimlessly and the quality of relationship you will have with him when he gets to the other side of his rebellious adventures.

Here's another thing I've found to be true. Most parents have done a good job developing their relationship with their child. The reason that you hurt over the current direction your teen has taken is probably because of the good relationship that you have with him. May I say that again? You hurt because you have had a good relationship with your son. That's why the way you treat him during the hard times will determine the quality of your relationship with him when he gets through it. Your homework tonight is to put this book down and write that a hundred times. Etch it into your mind and heart. It is critical during this time.

If you abandon your child when she struggles, you will lose the relationship you have fought so hard to build, and you will invalidate the truths you taught her. One of the greatest messages you can give your child is that she can do nothing to make you love her more, and she can do nothing to make you love her less. If you leave your daughter when she goes through a tough time—even if that tough time is excruciating for you—it sends the message that you love her only when she is doing well and not when she is not doing so well. I think we all understand that we're loved when we do great things, but deep in our hearts is a longing to know that we will receive that same love when we have done something wrong.

What kind of relationship would you have with me if I said, "I love you, but you'll lose that relationship if you do something wrong"? It's legalistic. It's performance-based. The expectations are too high. It's cheap, for anyone can love me when I do well. It's when I sin that I desperately want to know that I am loved. I have a feeling that you desire the same thing. I know your teen feels that way.

I can be disappointed in you for not fulfilling the dreams I have for you. But to lose the relationship? Uh-uh. If all your friends abandon you during your time of need, who's going to speak the truth to you during that dark time and bring you back into a better situation?

Deep down, don't you want someone to "cover your back," "go to bat for you," and "be there for you"? I'm sure you do.

But I know that your child's rebellion leaves you with a pretty big question: How do you love someone who is not following what she's been taught, is irresponsible, and has violated relationships, values, and the very principles you have built a relationship on? That's a tough one. "Tough love" isn't kicking your child out of the house, making her suffer consequences, and holding her to a strict set of standards that kicks in whenever she starts to do something wrong. That approach is really pretty easy in comparison to what I believe tough love really is. Tough love is loving your teen when she says she hates you, when she violates the very core of what you are all about, when she is intent on going against what you have taught her, and when she purposely pushes you to your limit and beyond. That's what tough love is. How do you love someone who is acting like that?

First, it's of utmost importance to remember that most teen rebellion and unsavory behavior is temporary. It's a bump in the road. It will end. It is a finite period of time that you will get to the other side of, short of your child dying because of his foolish choices. This less-than-desirable behavior won't last forever. This too shall pass.

A second vital thought for your family's existence during this time is that even though your teen is messing up, and regardless of how serious the behavior is, God has not abandoned you. Not only that, but He's going to use everything that is happening in the life of your teen to bring him to a better place. He really will use all things for good. Just because you can't see that right now doesn't mean that He isn't at work. God will fertilize the soil in which you have planted seeds. And fertilizer is usually stuff that stinks, that we'd just as soon not touch, and that we wash off of our shoes after we step in it. Yet from that fertilized soil comes growth, new life, and beauty as a result of your obedient planting of the seed and His fertilizing. Don't underestimate God's continual involvement in your situation. Even in silence, He is at work. He hasn't left you or your teen, and He never will.

Third, your role in this difficult time is to maintain the relationship, establish boundaries within your home, set the rules and consequences, quit enabling your child, let him assume responsibility for his actions, give him responsibility for his life, and quit rescuing him from everything. Is it going to be work to line these things out? You bet it is. But the result is worth the effort. And I think you will find a great sense of joy in watching God work in his life.

One night, I asked a group of teens living at Heartlight what they would want their parents to know about their rebellion. Their answers were insightful and shed a little light into their sometimes dark thinking. Here are a few of their responses:

- "Rebellion is a decision with a motive shown in behavior."

- "Rebellion can start as a response and then move to a choice of lifestyle if habits aren't broken."

- "It was fun, and I always had the feeling that the Lord would wait for me."

- "My rebellion was a cry for help."

- "Parents, be good role models. I used to think that what I was doing was okay because my mom used to do it."

- "I did things for attention."

- "My rebellious attitude got me the attention I never got any other way."

- "I wanted to pay back my parents for all the misery they caused in my life. The more intense it got at home, the better my plan was working."

- "I wasn't rebelling; I was just struggling."

- "My rebellion was my way of proving to my parents that I could be good at something because I was never good enough for them."

- "Rebellion is a response on steroids."

- "The one who goes into his room and listens to music to deal with his issues can be just as rebellious as the one who goes out and smokes dope."

- "I like fighting with my mom; it's the only time we talk or connect."

- "I love conflict. It is the time I get the most attention, we have the most discussion, and the focus is on me for once. It showed I was smart."

- "Rebellious actions don't mean that we don't love our parents."

- "I was so miserable that I wanted someone to experience it with me."

- "No matter how deep a hole I got into, I didn't want my parents to leave me."

These comments showed me that many of the choices these teens made that precipitated their rebellious times were intentional. I've given many different reasons for a teen's behavior, but I haven't given justification or license to any of them to continue to act out in hurtful ways. I may understand a teen's behavior, but that doesn't mean I agree with it. I can fully understand why a young man has chosen to escape pain in his life with the use of alcohol, but I don't agree with his choice to continue. My understanding of the situation allows me to approach the real issue in a way that embraces a relationship, affirms what I've taught, targets the real problem, and helps this young man move toward the place where he wants to be and away from a place where he doesn't want to be. My approach, my attitude, and my application of a process to help a young man like this is guided by my understanding of what is really happening in his life.

I must also understand that there are some things I can change and some things he must change. I can't make all the choices for him, I can only set up the best atmosphere possible for him to make good choices. Ultimately, he has to make the choice. I just want to make sure he isn't choosing poorly or making unwise decisions just to show me he is in control of his life. So many times, teens will choose badly to prove to their parents that they have control of their life.

I take parents through a process to reestablish their home, implement change, and avoid future conflict. That process will help them get their home in order and create an atmosphere that allows a teen to make choices, exercise his ability to take control of his life, and suffer the consequences and rewards of his choices. We determine what set the rebellion ball in motion. The teen's own choices then move him down the right or wrong path. This may be the beginning of maturity and responsibility for his own life—two qualities that we all want to see displayed before a teen heads off to college, gets married, or has kids.

Establish Boundaries

In our deepening relationships with our teens, many believe that parents are more like peers than they are parents. Many teens feel that they have equal ownership in their home, are equally entitled to everything in the home, and can have equal access to funds, time, and privileges. They feel this way because parents have raised them this way. The motive behind raising this way was to help them feel important, valuable, included, and blessed. But when they enter the teen years, it often backfires. These feelings can quickly turn into a great sense of entitlement, which creates a whole new world of disrespect for those who try to assume the role of authority within the home.

If this sounds like your home, it's time to teach your young children about boundaries so that when they become teens, they'll understand where they begin and where they end—and where you begin and where you end. They need to know what is theirs and what is not, what they are entitled to and what they are not entitled to. If you have not defined your role as a parent, they might not initially accept new boundaries. After all, those boundaries are likely to limit or restrict the privileges they have enjoyed in the past.

Ignore that initial negative response. Moms and dads, it's okay to say no. It's okay to set limits. It's okay not to do what you have always done. It fine to give some parameters. It's normal to take some time for yourself. It's okay to let your teens know what is no longer acceptable for you. It's okay to let them control their lives and not control yours. You must set some boundaries for yourself, or you will allow people, including your teens, to walk all over you. Walking with your teen is fun; being walked on is not.

Set Rules and Consequences

What ten things would you change in your home to make it run a little smoother and a little less chaotic? Write those ten things down. If disrespect is becoming an issue in your home, write down what you believe respect would look like, and put a rule in place that supports that belief. Then write down a consequence for a violation of that rule. It may look something like this:

> Belief: We believe that every person in our family should be treated with respect.
>
> Rule: Everyone in our family will speak with respect to each other, not violate personal space, and not act selfishly.
>
> Consequence: Any display of disrespect will result in the loss of privileges.

Consequences must be age-appropriate, configured to the workings of your family, specific to the issues in your family, and effective enough for your child to take notice and want to comply. I encourage parents to prioritize their rules from most important to least important and to couple the rules with consequences that their teen would rank similarly. In other words, if driving a car is currently the most important thing in your teen's life, then couple that privilege with the most important rule you have prioritized.

This is a very simple process. The hard part is to narrow down what you would like to see different in your home. You may be able to list a hundred things that you'd like to see changed. Whittle that list down to ten. If you list them all, you'll just be a "consequence policeman" and cease to be the mom or dad your child really needs. You can't correct everything, so pick the top ten and get those established. (I've written a workbook titled "Avoiding Conflict and Implementing Change" that helps parents use this process in their home. You can find information about this resource at www.HeartlightResources.com.)

Will your teens like this? Not in the short run, so expect some reaction or negative response. Very few people like change, and most teens don't want any restrictions. But some guidelines for the operation of your home will make for a happier setting for everyone in the long run.

Quit Giving Them Everything and Doing Everything for Them

We have given our kids everything, haven't we? The problem with allowing this habit of ours to continue past age 14 is that it keeps our children from wanting to do what is necessary to learn how to provide for themselves. I'm not suggesting that we stop giving our kids things cold turkey. But I am suggesting that we help them learn about limitations, finances, responsibility, and working. My fear for most families is that our expectations for our teens in these areas have been so low that they will have a tough time transitioning into marriage, once they strike out on their own.

Many teens have told me they could make it on their own, but when they tried to prove themselves right, they lost everything, got into trouble, and came home with their tails between their legs and a good lesson in their heart about their capabilities. The problem is that when parents give their teens everything, they create a false sense of independence that falls flat when reality strikes. One of the best things we can do for our teens is to require them to have a job where they get paid for doing work. They need to get paid by someone else, have another set of expectations to live up to, and learn some lessons from someone other than Mom and Dad.

At some point, quit doing their laundry. Allow them to run their own errands. Quit doing their homework research and writing their papers. Quit buying all their clothes. Quit paying for everything. Quit cleaning up every mess they make. Let them do all of these things and more. Perhaps the discomfort of having to clean up their own messes would help them stop the behavior that created the mess in the first place.

Quit Rescuing Them

If you rescue your child once, you'll have to rescue her again. If you're always making excuses for her and allowing her not to learn from the consequences of her actions, she is likely not to learn a lesson until a really big consequence comes along—one you can't rescue her from.

Allow consequences to have their full effect on your child. Spending a night in the county jail is far better for her than spending five years in prison. For her to pay for her speeding ticket and for the increased insurance premiums is better than for her to cause an accident. If your daughter gets arrested, make her do what is necessary to handle the legal trouble. If your son gets suspended from school, let him work it out.

As I said before, every responsibility you assume for your teen is one less responsibility he will have to accept and learn from. Every excuse you give for him is one less area of responsibility he will assume. By doing everything for him and rescuing him from all his foolish actions, you postpone his maturity and healthy development. You are setting your beloved son up for future failure. The goal of parenting is to give your teen the opportunity to be prepared to fulfill the expectations that will be made of him when he enters college, the job market, or a new role as a husband. What he doesn't learn now while living with you, he'll have to learn later when the consequences of ignorance are greater and more far-reaching.

When you sit down with your teens and explain to them that you want to establish some boundaries, set some rules and consequences, quit giving them everything and doing everything for them, and stop rescuing them, they'll probably look at you and think that you've lost it, or you are going through a midlife crisis, or—and this will be the scary one—you might be serious. You cannot begin to implement any of this without expecting a little conflict to result. Let me assure you, conflict is okay. You may not like it, but you can handle it. A little healthy conflict now to make changes sure beats a lot of unhealthy conflict later after the damage is done.

The worst that can happen is that your teens may tell you they are going to leave and that they can make it on their own. If your child is 13, she is probably just blowing smoke. If he is 17 or 18, he might just leave for a night. But change in your home is essential for your family to survive the adolescent years, so I encourage you to simply say, "We'll leave the light on for you."

This response will let your teen know he has some choices to make. It gives your son responsibility for his life. And it lets him know that he is always welcome in your home but that you are not going to be living as you have in the past. Your daughter must learn that she needs to develop responsibility and maturity. Better for her to learn that while she is with you and you can still daily speak truth in her life, than when she is out on her own, learning the hard way.

Chapter 21

Curious Actions Seldom Last

■ ■ ■ ■

The first time I saw two girls kissing was when I was growing up in New Orleans. I was with my brother and mom walking in the French Quarter close to Jackson Square. I remember my brother saying something like, "Look at that!" and out of the corner of my eye, I caught a glimpse of the two girls for just a second before my mom rushed to cover my eyes for fear that the sight might corrupt me and ruin my innocent youth.

A couple of years later, I was at a mall standing outside a pinball arcade (no minors allowed) when two girls walked out holding hands. A policeman nearby pointed at them and told them to quit. That was it. Those were the only two times I saw anything that resembled same-sex relationships. Then I moved to Oklahoma and forgot all about what I saw.

Yesterday, I saw wedding pictures of an afternoon talk-show host with her new partner in *People* magazine. Last night I watched a video of a young lady singing a song titled "I Kissed a Girl and I Liked It." (At the time, it was one of the top-ten downloaded songs on iTunes.) And when Madonna and Britney Spears kissed on the 2003 MTV Video Music Awards, what had remained hush-hush for years was now broadcast to ten million teen viewers and became the talk of millions more the next day.

Whenever I'm with a group of teens, I ask questions to find out what they're thinking and what's happening in their world. I throw out idea after idea and bounce thoughts around to see how world happenings and cultural changes are affecting them. When I ask them what they think about girls kissing girls, most say that it doesn't bother them. "If they want to do that, it's their life." When I ask if they have any gay friends, most say, "Yeah, but it's not that big of a deal." When I ask girls if it would bother their future boyfriends if they've kissed a girl before, some answer, "Not at all. He'd probably like it." It's a heck of a way to start up a conversation with teens.

I was driving a group of our Heartlight girls to Starbucks following a hot and humid morning of riding horses. We needed to take a break and cool off before we turned the horses out to pasture. While we were driving into town, one of the girls asked, "Mark, you're always asking us questions. Can I ask you one?"

I answered, "Sure, ask anything you want."

She asked, "If you came home and found Jan in bed with someone, would you rather it be a man or a woman?"

I was stunned. I was shocked. I was speechless. Not because I didn't have an answer, but because I had no idea I would be asked a question of this nature, and even more because I had no idea that some girls were thinking about this. Needless to say, our discussion at Starbucks was pretty eye-opening. I quit saying "Sure, ask me anything you want."

I mention all this to highlight the sexual flavor of today's culture that our young ladies, your teens, are growing up in. It's truly a mixed bag. It's not just the ol' guy-girl relationships they have always wrestled with. Now our teens are surrounded by a confused mixture of relationships, a continual changing of partners, and highly publicized relationship fiascos. The sexualization of young girls by our society and the enormous amount of exposure that these girls have to various types of relationships is overwhelming.

So to think that your daughter is not going to be affected in some way might be to underestimate the power of the culture's influence on her. You might be overestimating your daughter's ability to remain unscathed by her exposure. I have seen young ladies from the finest of families, with the finest biblical upbringing, who are great kids with great values and a great future, get sidetracked and confused by same-sex relationships. Every single one of their moms and dads who have asked for my help said they had no idea that their daughter would engage in a same-sex relationship.

A loving dad told me yesterday that he about got sick when his daughter who was off at college mentioned to him that she had just broken up with her girlfriend. He said that if someone told him a few years ago that his daughter would have a girlfriend her senior year of college, he would have told him he was absolutely crazy. He now thinks he is going crazy with the thought of this being a possibility for his daughter.

When Mark called me, he was in tears. He was lost, having just been blindsided by journal entries in Emily's diary that turned his world upside down. He read of sexual trysts, affectionate encounters, and intimate words between his daughter and another girl just one year older. The two girls had known each other for years, but they "got together" on the church mission trip when they roomed together. The youth minister and his wife said they had seen nothing and didn't suspect any type of wrong behavior as they reflected back on the trip.

Mark's wife suspected something when Emily's friend spent the night and the mom went up to tell the girls good-night. The look of guilt in her daughter's eyes tweaked this mother's sixth sense, and she knew something was wrong. She thought they were in the shower together the next morning when she went up to make sure they had gotten out of bed. She shared her concerns with Mark, and he then decided to do some detective work.

He reviewed all her text messages and became alarmed. He looked at her MySpace account with a different perspective and began to read Emily's comments a little differently. He searched for reasons to disqualify his worst fears but could only validate what he suspected. He snooped and sought out any type of conversation between his daughter and her friend, and what he found made him sick.

Mark is my age and grew up in a world where this type of behavior meant only one thing. In his anger and disappointment, he confronted the girls one morning as they sat at the breakfast table. He labeled them lesbians, called them sinful, expelled the friend from the house, and grounded his daughter from school until she could promise that she would never see this girl again. The yelling and screaming that ensued only inflamed the issue and brought in the other family members, who shamed their sister and cursed her actions and behavior.

Do I need to tell you it was a mess? It always is. Mark got my name from someone who had heard me on the radio. I flew to meet him and his wife with hopes of helping them understand their daughter and helping their daughter understand them.

Mark never thought Emily would move in the direction she did or engage in the activities she was involved in, so he had never had discussions about same-sex relationships. As a matter of fact, he didn't know anything about same-sex relationships except for those that carried labels like *fag, homo, gay, lesbian,* and *dyke.* Like any father, he feared the worst and let his imagination take him to a dark place. He was angry, his wife became depressed, and his family was thrown into turmoil.

Mark had always thought that if he just did the right things, his daughter would always walk a straight path. You know the drill. Teach her Scripture. Take her to church. Spend time with her. Let her know she is loved. Take her places. Give her a good life. Be a good father. Help her do the things she wanted to do. Provide activities and opportunities. Build into her some scriptural principles and good morals. Mark thought that if he did those things, everything would work our right. The problem was that this loving father underestimated the power of today's culture and the pull it had on his daughter. Because he thought this would never happen, he never prepared. And now, with Emily already engaged in behavior he had not even imagined, Mark didn't know what to do, where to turn, what to say, how to act, or why this was all happening. He felt lost, alone, and hopeless.

I don't mean to shock you, but Mark's situation with his daughter is not that abnormal anymore. This culture affects all teens; no teen is immune to its allure. I explained to Mark and his wife that curiosity and experimentation are far different from an intentional choice to adopt a new lifestyle. After I met with his daughter, I was convinced that her involvement was more of the former than the latter. Let me explain why I came to that conclusion.

Mark and his wife had raised their daughter in a pretty strict environment. They did much for her and required much from her. They allowed her to do quite a bit with the church, but outside of those privileges, activities were pretty limited. They didn't allow her to date, she couldn't talk to guys on the phone, and she wasn't allowed to go to dances, hang out at the popular places, or stay out late with her friends. They required her to dress modestly, she couldn't see movies that were rated above PG, and they didn't think she should drive quite yet, even though she was 16 and all her friends drove.

I'm not saying the restrictions that Mark and his wife placed on their daughter were wrong. But their choices for Emily made it hard for her to engage with her peers. The lifestyle her parents imposed wasn't wrong; it was just hard. She felt limited from relationships with guys and restricted in her relationships with girls too. She always felt unattached and unloved, and she longed for a connection with someone.

Along came a culture of curiosity and a readily available option. She knew that others had experimented and lived to tell of their escapades. Other girls talked about it. In the lunchroom at school, some girls shared their experiences, and Emily found herself wondering, *What is this about?* Her curiosity had been stirred.

She noticed other girls holding hands. She saw pictures of girls kissing in the newspaper. She listened to songs about girls being together. She heard guys joke about it. The prevalence of same-sex relationships was all around. And as with any other teen on the face of the earth, the more she saw it, the more she got used to it.

When Emily saw that celebrities had this type of relationship, she felt she had permission to experiment. The combination of her curiosity, the prevalence of same-sex experimentation in her community, and the permissiveness of her culture all came together to create the perfect opportunity for a problem when Emily was paired to room with this girl she had known for years on this mission trip.

Emily told me that through all of the sexual escapades she experienced with her girlfriend, she never thought of it as having sex. She talked of affection and connection and never thought she was violating a vow she had made to her dad and to God to remain pure until she got married. She wanted to get married, have kids, and live happily ever after. She never thought she was a lesbian, never considered that she was gay, and in a weird way, thought her relationship didn't violate anything she had been taught. That was actually a true statement because she never had been taught anything about this area. Her mom and dad never imagined they needed to teach on this subject.

I'm not going to go into all the details of the enticements for girls to have a same-sex relationship because I would have to write another 500 pages. But I will tell you that a needy girl who is given permission by the current culture to calm her curiosity through experimentation just might do so. I was convinced that Emily was drawn into this relationship for a number of factors, and her parents were at a loss because they never knew they would have to tackle such an issue.

So what are parents to do when they find their daughter in a same-sex relationship? Here's the approach that I encourage parents to take.

Dispel Your Anger and Release Your Rage

Anger will tear you up if you don't let it go. No parent wants to hear this news about his daughter. A same-sex relationship is so foreign to an older culture that most parents wonder where they went wrong or how crazy their child must be. I would challenge both those thoughts. I don't think you have gone wrong, even though you may not have done everything right, and I don't think your teen is crazy. I believe your daughter has been led astray and enticed into something that is permissible in her culture.

The way you respond to your daughter's same-sex relationship will greatly affect the amount of time that she remains in her inappropriate behavior. Pushing her away, fueling her anger, and condemning her will only push her back to the person she feels cares about her—the one she has shared an intimate relationship with. The intimacy of a relationship will bond people together regardless of gender. So be careful in your approach.

Take your anger before the Lord and ask Him to calm your heart as you engage in the battle before you. And take time to think this through before you confront your daughter. If this relationship has been going on for a while, waiting a couple of weeks to begin discussions probably isn't going to hurt anything. Holding off on consequences, limitations, or restrictions might work better for the situation in the long run. If you run straight into your daughter's room the moment after your discovery to tell her that you know what's been going on and that she's grounded for life, you will make the situation worse. So give yourself some time. Make sure you're not angry or worn out when you confront her.

I can assure you that this hurdle will test your patience, your faith in God, and your confidence in who you are as a parent. But this is the time you have been practicing for all your life. Be slow to speak, slow to anger, and quick to listen. Your approach will make a difference in the way your daughter responds, so approach wisely. One difficult aspect of the situation is her deceitfulness. She had to be deceitful because somewhere inside she knew what she was doing was wrong. Her internal moral compass is evidently still working, and that is a good sign. She understands what she is doing is wrong, or she wouldn't have any reason to hide her actions.

Get over your hurt first and then confront your daughter—not to stop your pain, but to help her get to a better place. Remember, your goal is to help her, not just to point out her sinful behavior. Consider honestly whether your daughter's actions are an attempt to get back at you for something in your relationship that has hurt her. Ask yourself if you can think of any reason why she would want to hurt you or pay back anyone in the family. Do your homework, and don't leave any stones unturned. The more you know about what is driving your child into this relationship, the better off you'll be when you begin having conversations with her.

Talk to Your Daughter One-on-One

Once you make the discovery, ask your daughter to talk with one parent, not both at once. Don't let her feel as if you are ganging up on her. Your daughter has moved in the direction she has because of a need. Spend some time trying to find out what that need is. She's found something she likes in this girlfriend. What is it? That will be a key component in trying to steer her away from this relationship. When you sit down to talk, help her to take these messages to heart:

- "We love you, and nothing can make us love you less or make us love you more."

- "I'd like for you to tell me about this relationship and what you see it as."

- "I want you to know that I don't think you're gay just because of this relationship."

- "I'd like for us to get together once a week to talk about what's going on in your life."

- "Your mother (or father) and I love you. We always will."

When you ask honest and open questions about inappropriate behavior, you'll probably hear about how many communication lines are *not* there and how you have failed your teen in some way. Keep your focus. Admit where you have failed. Accept responsibility where you have been wrong. And encourage more discussion. Don't expect everything to be resolved in one conversation. Your task at this first meeting is to find out where she is in this relationship.

Set Some Parameters on the Relationship

To allow the same sex-relationship to continue just because you now understand how your daughter got there would be ludicrous. At some point, perhaps when the anger has calmed and you've had time to sit down and talk, you can share with her what you will allow and what you won't. When parents ask what to allow, I ask them if they would allow their daughter to be involved in an opposite-sex relationship to the same degree.

At some point, you will have to determine if this relationship is one of curiosity and convenience and just a passing thing, or if it is one that is going to last. Not all these relationships lead to an alternative lifestyle. But some do, and because of your daughter's choice and her age, you may not be able to do much about it. The younger your teen, the more you can control. The older the teen, the less you can control.

When you have released your anger, talked to your daughter, and set some parameters on the relationship, you are now at first base. You have a long way to go. There are no quick and easy answers. Find someone who can walk with you as the situation unfolds. You need someone to talk to and walk with as you travel this path. You will learn things you've never known before, and you'll experience God's comfort as never before.

Even if your daughter continues on this path of same-sex relationship, she needs to know of your love for her and the longing in your heart for good things for her. But you also have to deal with the behavior at hand. Once you've talked with your daughter and made a decision, act quickly and decisively. A daughter might respond to your conversation in a positive way, admitting that what's been going on is wrong and showing a desire to turn from this relationship.

Or she might fight you, stating that you can't tell her what to do, that she'll continue in the relationship, and that you can't control her. If this is the case, you definitely have a problem. If your daughter is under 17, I would encourage you to do whatever you have to do to get her away from this relationship. Change her school, remove her communication devices, or even move away. Again, what would you do if your daughter was having an unacceptable relationship with a young man? She has more access to this girl than to guys.

Get counsel from a trusted person, and get your daughter to a counselor as one condition of your future support of her chosen lifestyle. Even though most of these same-sex, faddish relationships are born out of personal curiosity and cultural acceptance don't ignore the impact or potential personal damage of the relationship if it continues. Love does strange things in the heart of a young woman, and even stranger things when the object of her love is of the same sex, regardless of how she got there.

Chapter 22

It's All in the Approach

■ ■ ■ ■

When Frank called me last week, I was at home watching the springboard diving event of the Beijing 2008 Olympics. I dove competitively during my swimming years until I had an accident and cracked my head open on a trampoline. While trying to do a couple of flips, my approach was wrong, my legs came down too soon, and my knee split my head from my nose up to my hairline. That one bad experience scared me to death, shut down my diving career, and gave me a deeper appreciation for those who compete. As I watched the diving event, I kept hearing the commentators say that the heart of any dive was all in the approach.

Frank called frantically a couple of weeks ago, looking for ways to deal with his 16-year-old son. His son had recently driven home drunk and thrown up all over the inside of the car. Frank and his son had always gotten along, but Frank suspected that his son had started experimenting with alcohol, and this Saturday night's escapade validated his suspicions. His son violated his curfew that night, consumed alcohol (which he knew was against the rules), acted irresponsibly, put other people's lives in danger, stunk up his dad's car, and ignored his dad's questions when he returned home late. Frank told him to go to his room upon his return home and stated that they would talk in the morning. Needless to say, Frank didn't sleep much that night, and his blood pressure soared. His anger and concern had him tied in knots.

The next morning, Frank went to his son's room, woke him up, told him to get downstairs, and proceeded to let him have it. Frank made accusations about his stupid immaturity, his lack of reasoning, his selfish behavior, his lack of respect for the family, his unrepentant attitude, his refusal to look Frank in the eyes, his self-centered attitude for not getting up and cleaning out the car (which Frank had already done), Frank's disappointment in him, how embarrassed his mother was going to be, and how he was setting a bad example for his younger brothers and sisters. How dare he, in the sight of God, live a hypocritical life?

Frank was intense. He yelled. He screamed a few times. He pounded the table and woke everyone else up in the house. Then Frank stormed out of the house in anger. His son just sat and took it all in, listening deeply to Frank and silently controlling his building rage.

Now, a week later, Frank's wife was still upset at him for the way he handled his son. The other children have said that Dad was too harsh, and Frank's son has graciously accepted the consequences of losing his driving privileges. But his son hasn't said a word to him since the morning of Frank's rant, and Frank called me, wanting some advice about what to do.

It's All in the Approach

Frank's approach was abrupt. He did a cannonball on his son, jack-knifed the family into anger, and created a Shamu-sized splash that drenched everyone in the family. I'd say Frank scored about a 2.5 on a scale of 1 to 10. He wasn't going to win this competition. As a matter of fact, the whole family lost because of Frank's approach.

I told Frank that his son was wrong in his actions but that Frank was equally wrong in his reaction. Two wrongs never make a right, and Frank's rant took the focus off his son's wrong behavior. But Frank was defensive in his conversation with me, and he couldn't let go of the idea that he was right. He kept saying, "I'm not wrong; it was my son who was wrong." I kept telling him that no one was saying his son wasn't wrong, but Frank just couldn't accept the fact that neither of them had handled things well. I told Frank that his "approach needed to be above reproach." He didn't get it. He never called back. I thought about Frank as I watched the closing ceremonies of the Olympics, which highlighted a number of people who had medaled in diving. They went home winners because they had the right approach.

What's the Right Approach?

I've said many times that I believe teens should suffer the consequences of their choices. I'm a stickler for making sure they assume responsibility for their actions, learn from their mistakes, and feel the results of their decisions. But I'm not going to talk about those things in this chapter. I want to detail here a way that parents can approach their teen who has done something wrong. How can they dive into the life of their teen in the precise spot where it's needed with as little splash possible, regardless of the degree of difficulty the offense has created?

Step Up on the Right Board:
Understand That Conflict Can Be a Good Thing

As we have already seen, conflict can be a sign of something very good. For most parents, recognizing the good that can result from conflict requires a huge shift in their perspective. Most parents try not to rock the boat; they work to preserve an old way of operation that is no longer working or effective. But conflict can be an opportunity to fight for positive changes in your teen's life. Don't be afraid of the springboard of conflict. It can launch you into new ways to help your teen change what is wrong and to encourage him to learn from his mistakes. But your teen isn't the only one who needs to make some changes.

Most people hate change. The thought of making changes at home is scary and challenging. Parents who climb up on the springboard of conflict commit to two things: confronting those areas that need change in the life of their teen, and facing the areas in their own lives that need to change. To start requiring changes in a son or daughter's life without being willing to introspectively look at your own life would be hypocritical.

If parents don't make the needed changes in their lives before they require changes in the life of their child, they will not get the "bounce" they need to get the most out of their conflict. If you find yourself in a difficult time with your teen right now, remember that even your best parenting didn't prevent the situation. So something has to change. As M. Craig Barnes states in his book *Sacred Thirst*, "It always amazes me, but I've seen all too often that people prefer the misery they know to the mystery they do not."

Neither teens nor parents really understand what's on the other side of these adolescent years. But to remain in the difficult position many parents find themselves in, thinking that everything will change with time, without diving into conflict and doing the hard work of changing is foolish. Granted, if parents don't make any changes in their lives but just allow time to pass, their teen may eventually mature and could grow out of his inappropriate behavior. But the relationship between parent and child may not improve. In fact, when parents don't change, the relationship usually deteriorates even more. Unless all parties change—parents as well as teens—they will probably lose something precious.

I've had the honor to perform more than four hundred weddings, and I've seen all types. Most of the weddings I have performed have been for adults I spent time with back when they struggled through their teen years. And I can tell you that in the most joy-filled wedding celebrations, the bride or groom was once a teen who had huge struggles, but the parents hung in there and made changes in their own lives as well. These weddings are fun, celebratory, exciting, and worshipful experiences because everyone can see how God has guided this family toward restored relationships. When a wedding takes place some time after a family has struggled with really hard things, and everyone has done the tough work necessary to make positive changes in their relationships, the event celebrates not only the joining of two people but also the mighty power of God and His faithfulness to get the whole family, including Mom and Dad, to the other side of the adolescent years.

Many times when parents come to my seminars, write in questions to our radio program, come to retreats I lead, or seek counsel for their situation at home, they are looking for one of two things: more ammunition to use against their spouse or teen to defend their own actions, or more justification for what they're doing or thinking. Neither of these is productive. If these parents are successful in accomplishing what they came to do—avoid having to make any personal changes—their failed method will continue the family's downward spiral. Proverbs tells us, "The way of a fool seems right to him" (Proverbs 12:15). This verse is not only a description of a fool, it is also a good check for parents who choose to handle the situation with their teen in the same old ways.

Change needs to happen in your family. Frank needed to change his approach. His anger erupted whenever his children made mistakes. When Frank got mad, he exploded, which only fueled the crisis and steered it away from resolution. Frank also had a tendency to dump on his kids whenever they did something wrong, yet Frank couldn't take criticism himself. The areas of change needed in a parent's life usually surface when conflict is in the home. That's why people feel as if everything is falling apart when they are struggling with just one teen. It's not that "when it rains, it pours"; it's just that other stuff comes out. That's what happened with Frank.

If you are parents of preteens, your parenting style will need to shift to accommodate the new needs of your budding teen. If you are parents of teens and you're experiencing some difficulty at the moment, you may need to change some things in your own life. You can change only two things that affect your teen: yourself and the atmosphere of your home. But those two changes are powerful and attractive to teens, and they can lead to change in the life of your child.

To think that you can actually change your teen is foolishness. Your attempts to do so will be futile and probably harmful. Teens must make a decision to change and then make the right choices to follow through on that change. But you can show them how by making changes yourself.

Don't Dive into Unknown Water: Understand the World's Influence on Your Teen

The apostle Paul writes, "See that no one takes you captive through hollow and deceptive philosophy, which depends on human tradition and the basic principles of this world rather than on Christ" (Colossians 2:8). Did you ever think that your daughter would be deceived or taken captive by philosophies and principles that are contrary to your beliefs and her upbringing? Welcome to the real world! You'll engage the battle within your home, around the dinner table, while driving in your car, at odd hours of the day and night, and in uncomfortable conversations that will challenge your thinking and confuse your wits. This encounter might last months at best and years at worst. It will change your plans and disrupt your agenda. It will cramp your style, keep you from fulfilling some of your dreams, and cause you to put some things on the back burner. I encourage you to approach the fight in the most godly way you can.

You're going to have to drop some things and get focused on the real issues at hand. You might have to invest some time that you don't have, spend some money that you've been saving, change your schedule, and adapt to some of your son's real needs right now. Albert Einstein once said, "Not everything that counts can be counted, and not everything that can be counted counts." Let me share something with you—this counts.

Your teen is growing up in a tough culture. I hear parents say daily how they are glad that they don't have to grow up in this environment. Much of what this culture is throwing at our teens is beyond our wildest imaginations. I never thought 20 years ago that we'd be talking about same-sex relationships, oral sex on the playground, the seduction of our young teen girls, instant pornography, digital transfer of pictures and messaging, Internet networking, sex with teachers, and today's attitudes of disrespect, mind-sets of entitlement, and demands for instant gratification. Did you picture this scenario 20 years ago? It's caught us all off guard. Not just Christians, but all of us. And teens are caught off guard as well. But they don't know a world that's any different, and they don't have the social support of the principles their parents have taught them. So we as parents, youth ministers, pastors, and teachers have to be the ones who help them understand the difference.

It's a tough place for teens to be. Some of the responses we see from our teens are results of the culture's influence on them. It can be a dark hole that swallows them up. Knowing this, our responses back to them should be seasoned with understanding and compassion. They don't need our angry demands to straighten up and fly right. Frank, in his good intention of confronting his son about something that was way out of bounds for their family, forgot to ask the questions about why it happened. He never asked if a friend had died, if something was troubling his son, or what else was going on. He never looked beyond the behavior to uncover some deeper issues that might have been lurking. His son may have experienced something traumatic that day, or he may have just made a mistake.

Let's not treat our teens as the enemy. They are not. They are influenced by our enemy. They are not against you. They are not rejecting everything you've taught them. You might be thinking, *You have no idea what I'm going through! It sure feels like they are rejecting everything I hold dear. My daughter is sneaking out at night, is sexually active with a young man, and is beginning to drink and party.* I would tell you again, she is being influenced by a social culture that is giving her permission and license to do these things and is encouraging her to do what she wants. She has succumbed to a deceitful philosophy and is being enticed by the principles of the world, not those of Christ. My explanation does not support her activities, nor does it lessen the need for consequences, restrictions, limits, and boundaries in her life. But it should emphasize the need for love, compassion, empathy, mercy, grace, and understanding to go hand in hand with limits.

Season your approach with love—and don't walk away! Be there for your teen through thick and thin, when times are good and times are bad, and when the situations don't always look like what you had planned.

Stay Focused—This Issue Is About Them

The way you respond to your teen is the key at this point. Don't increase your child's anger and stubbornness by fighting. Heated discussions and arguments can easily lead away from the intended message. Don't let your response to your teen become a bigger issue than what your teen is facing. Get out of the way and allow the issues at hand, your *teen's* issues, be your focus. Make sure your approach is above reproach. If you yell and scream, your teen tunes out. You become a jerk rather than your teen's guide out of a bad situation. When you get on the springboard of conflict, know what you're up there for, what to do, and how to approach the opportunity in such a way that it keeps the focus on your teen, not on you.

I quoted Albert Einstein earlier. He was a much smarter man than I am, and I bet he understood parent-teen conflicts. He states, "Any intelligent fool can make things bigger and more complex. It takes a touch of genius...and a lot of courage to move in the opposite direction." Parents show a touch of genius when they don't exacerbate the issues, making them larger than they are. Wise parents make the issues smaller and the heart and health of the teen of bigger importance.

Your goal is to help your child. Your motive, focus, and mind-set should be about your teen—helping her get to a better place than where she is, and keeping her from a place she doesn't want to end up. This is not a time for you to make a statement; it is an opportunity to touch the heart of your child. It is not the time for you to unleash your anger and disappointment; it is a time to move into a deeper relationship with your child. This is not about you; this is about your teen. So work hard to keep the focus on your child. Paul said it best: "Do nothing out of selfishness ambition or vain deceit, but in humility consider others better than yourselves. Each of you should look not only to you own interests, but also to the interests of others" (Philippians 2:3-4).

Be Gentle in Your Approach

Do you think your response to your teen's issues will make a difference in their resolution? Consider this Scripture: "And the Lord's servant must not quarrel; instead, he must be kind to everyone, able to teach, not resentful. Those who oppose him he must gently instruct, in the hope that God will grant them repentance leading them to a knowledge of the truth, and that they will come to their senses and escape from the trap of the devil, who has taken them captive to do his will" (2 Timothy 2:24-26).

Do you see any merit in changing your approach to your teen who is struggling as you try to move him to a different place? Might this Scripture be written to you? These phrases touch the parenting side of me with comments like "not resentful," "gently instruct," "escape from the trap of the devil," and (here's the big one) "come to their senses." Does that last phrase sound familiar? It's in the story of the prodigal son in Luke 15:17. You can help your son come to his senses. And you can keep him from putting all the blame and responsibility for his situation on you.

How? With gentleness. Even if he has thrown up in your car, your gentle answer can turn away wrath (Proverbs 15:1). It's takes two to tango, so don't. Affirm your relationship with your child, get to the heart of the matter, and allow the consequences to do their job. Don't give in. Stay focused on what your teen needs. Admit fault and your own wrongdoing and remember that it's all in the approach.

Chapter 23

When "Abnormal" Is Their "Normal"

■ ■ ■ ■

A dear friend was telling me about his daughter and the struggles he and his wife were experiencing with her after adopting her at an older age. They had read all the books, done all the research, talked to wise friends, and attended a couple of seminars about adopting older kids. They wanted to know what issues they were going to have to tackle, what problems might arise, and how to deal with potential areas of conflict. He stated that they were well-versed, prepared, and ready to tackle this next chapter of their life.

He also stated that the minute they walked into their home after trekking halfway across the world to pick up their new daughter, they felt lost and helpless. He said, "All the books, seminars, and research told us about the abnormal things we would face. They didn't tell us that what they considered abnormal, she considered normal. It's been miserable since the day we brought her home, for us and for her."

That statement has stuck with me through the years and has shaped my approach to teens and parents who feel lost and helpless. A deeper understanding of what you're dealing with and an awareness of the pressures that are normal for your teen can help you keep your sanity and help your teen through a difficult time.

I've mentioned that when parents are confronted with behavior that is puzzling and unacceptable, they should look at what is fueling the need for such behavior. I've encouraged you to look below the surface. You must see with the eyes of your heart what is really going on. With one eye, look below the surface of your teen's behavior, and with the other eye, look around and see the world the way your teen sees it. This combination might give you a better perspective of what is really happening in the life of your teen.

Most problems with teens begin to show themselves in the school setting. It is the first time that kids are required to behave in a certain way, meet certain expectations of performance, learn in a particular style, respect another authority, sit and focus, control their behavior, and engage with others socially. Most kids adapt, fit in, and survive the education process. But far too many don't do well in that setting, and teachers tend to mark them as "problem kids" just because they don't fit into the educational system. Standardized methods of teaching and testing are wonderful indicators of the effectiveness of the system but not always of the capability of the students. The school system can become a nightmare for some kids. When a child doesn't fit into the school system, the problem may not lie with the child. The system might not be able to adapt to his unique needs.

A school administrator once told me that the kids who live with us at Heartlight and attend the local high school were not welcome in his school system unless 80 percent of them could pass a standardized test required by the state. Can you believe that? I was shocked and as angry as I have ever been. Our kids weren't welcome if they couldn't reach a certain level. I know the system has to operate, but I also know about those who struggle. When a teen is struggling with life and we're struggling to make sure this child survives, a standardized test is the least of our worries. I tell educators all the time that I understand their needs. I just ask that they understand the needs of those who don't always see eye to eye with their expectations.

Take a look at the school setting through a teen's eyes, and get a glimpse of what he sees and why he needs his parents to have vision of a different sort.

Danny's parents separated when he was in the seventh grade. They became so consumed with their divorce and nasty court proceedings in the years that followed that Danny had to meet his own needs for nurture, relationship, and guidance. So that's exactly what he did. He attached to older kids and naturally started doing things older kids do. When his mother tried to corral his activities, Danny, desperate for relationship, rebelled. His focus at school became more social than academic. He was tardy to classes because he was a social butterfly. He was late to school regularly because he lived as a 16-year-old on his own and didn't have all the kinks of following a schedule worked out. He flunked a few classes along the way, became independent early in life, and didn't want anyone telling him what to do because he had learned to live on his own.

When Danny came to live with us, he was angry whenever someone told him what to do. His flunking, tardiness, rebellion, and argumentativeness got him expelled from school and ultimately from his home. I think he deserved a medal for surviving the way he did.

We were out riding horses one afternoon when Danny made a profound statement: "You know, Mark, there wouldn't be anything wrong with what I'm doing if I was just two years older." He was right, and I told him so. But I also told him that my job was to ensure that he was going to be around in two years.

When he graduated from college, he sent me a letter that he had sent to all his high school teachers. It was to help them see that they didn't help him one bit, never bent over backward for him. His college diploma was a symbol of their inability to help a kid in need. Was he bitter? Yes, just a little. But as time passed, he moved on, forgot about all the hardship in his life, and is now a proud husband and father.

Michael smiled all the time. I mean, all the time. He smiled when he was laughing, when he was crying, and to his misfortune, when he was being corrected for his wrongdoings. The "smirk on his face" that he could never wipe away constantly got him into trouble. Teachers didn't like correcting him and seeing him smile back at them. What was interpreted as rebellion was nothing more than a normal response from a happy-go-lucky kid. The teachers' label of "rebellious" landed Michael in the in-school suspension setting numerous times. His inability to show regret and repentance extended his short-term sentences and caused many teachers not to want him in their classrooms. This type of behavior did not make a good example. It just wasn't normal for kids to smile at their teachers when being corrected. But it was for Michael.

Chris was a dorky kid. Bless his heart, if an accident was going to happen, he was usually the cause. If something went wrong, he was more than likely in the middle of it. If someone was pulling stupid stunts, Chris was showing his leadership abilities. He was so desperate to engage with people that he never quit talking, always tried to impress those around him, and was just an immature kid. The ridicule of his peers just drove him more. The rejection from the same group made him try harder. He was obnoxious in his comments, goofy in his questions and answers, and odd in his approach. He was a high-maintenance kid who became a high-maintenance teen. When he was kicked out of his Christian school, he felt rejected not only by the people he tried to love but also by God.

When Chris was finally diagnosed with an impulsive disorder and treated medically, he made progress and began to grow in new ways. But he still grew away from God, away from school, and away from all those who ridiculed him.

Kara reluctantly followed a couple of older guys out to their car in the parking lot to look at the car's sound system. The older boys said that what followed was consensual; she said it was rape. The school said she chose to go out to the car and that they could do nothing about it. In the car, she was forced to do something she didn't want to do. And at school, she was forced to face these two boys and the ridicule of her peers.

I wasn't surprised when her parents said she was depressed and didn't want to go to school. I wasn't surprised that she became quiet, withdrawn, and a loner. I wasn't surprised when she gave up her church, her family, and her friends. All this sounded like a pretty normal response to the situation to me.

Chad couldn't sit in a classroom setting for the whole 90-minute class time. He grew fidgety, couldn't concentrate, and never performed at the level of the other kids. Whenever teachers posted grades on the board, everyone knew that Chad's scores would be on the bottom. He knew that he just didn't think like the rest of his friends, and he felt abnormal. But that was normal to him. He once told me that high school was "everything I am not, trying to make me into someone I will never be, and always telling me I'm a failure." He exploded when he was put in special education classes that lumped him in with a bunch of what he said were "retarded kids who rode the short bus." He did not see himself as abnormal.

I wasn't surprised when Chad started using drugs. He said they eased the feelings of being labeled as abnormal. And I wasn't surprised when his mother told me that he had dropped out of school. Chad told me that he'd rather be stupid and happy than smart and sad. I told him his comments were a normal response to what he had been through. Do you want to know what his comment back to me was? "That's the first time anyone has ever said there was something normal about me." When he lived with us and finally graduated from high school, he hugged my neck and said, "I finally feel normal."

I told him, "You always have been, Chad."

I'm not saying school administrators should adjust every academic system to accommodate every child. That would be impossible. But if you have a teen who is struggling in that particular setting, here are some positive ideas that might help counter some of the negative effects of a system that tends to label a child and begin a snowball of negativity that is hard to stop.

First, learn to adjust your expectations about what you want *for* your teen and what you want *from* your teen. Adjust until neither you nor your teen is frustrated all the time.

For example, you might have to accept the fact that high school is going to be a bumpy few years. You might have to learn to celebrate maintenance rather than performance. That maintenance might entail damage control, finishing the high school education, and restoring and maintaining the relationship with your teen.

Second, provide a home that feels normal for your teen. Looking through their child's eyes, parents can tweak their level of boundaries, rules, and consequences to fit the needs of their child and their home. When parents understand the true issues they are dealing with, they are usually a little more willing to accommodate a child who has not chosen all the issues he possesses. They lower their expectations so they can maintain relationships and order in the home.

Third, spend some time determining the best course of study for your child. He may be in the wrong school. I would never label a child a "problem child" as much as I would label a school a "problem school" for a particular child. The school can withstand such a label and continue fine. A child or teen cannot. Make sure your teen understands that school issues have more to do with the school's inability to meet your teen's needs than your teen's inability to measure up to the school's expectations. Plenty of magnet schools, alternative schools, Christian schools, and other public schools are available that could give your child an education without making him feel abnormal. Homeschooling, assisted learning opportunities, and charter schools are great alternatives. Let your child be a part of that process, and after visiting all the alternatives, let him pick which one he feels would be right for him. Letting him make a decision about where to be schooled places on him the responsibility to live up to the choices he makes, and that is always a good lesson to learn.

Fourth, outside help is always a good resource. A concerned youth minister, a friend who understands and has a connection with your teen, and a counselor who can give some wise and appropriate reflection are good alternatives to your teen only and always hearing counsel from you. Your teen needs to be affirmed.

I worked with a counselor on my own issues for months. I'll never forget the day she said, "You have every right to feel the way you do." Those words were a tremendous relief. They affirmed that some of my feelings and thoughts were not abnormal and that I really was quite normal. This pivotal point in my life helped me make great strides toward a healthier self-image amid my attention deficit issues, my struggles of the past, and my concept of myself and the people around me.

Finally, if behaviors have become dangerous, the issues your teen is displaying carry some pretty big consequences, and you have exhausted all the other resources, get your child to a safe place. If outside counseling is not working and all your attempts to control issues within your home have failed, get help elsewhere, even if it means having your child live with another family member where she can receive the help she needs, or in a residential counseling program like Heartlight where she is safe.

Ignoring bad behavior today only means that you're going to have to deal with a bigger problem later. Issues, hurts, losses, and pain don't usually go away with the mere passage of time. Oh, they might be covered up and hidden, but issues of earlier years usually reappear at significant stress points later in life—when your grown teen goes off to college, gets a job, gets married, begins to have children of her own, or moves to a new city.

What you work through now with your teen is one less thing she will have to work through when she has a new roommate, either in college or in marriage. Don't make her carry her issues and mistakes into the next significant relationships. Your commitment to work through areas that need attention now will affect your grandchildren. I tell people all the time that if they like their kids, they're going to love their grandchildren, so your investment in your child's life will greatly affect the future people in your life.

My prayer for you is from Ephesians 1:18, a verse that the apostle Paul wrote: "I pray also that the eyes of your heart may be enlightened in order that you may know the hope to which He has called you." Look with the eyes of your heart! You'll see a side of your teen that will draw you closer to him and help you to say, "Regardless of what happens, I will always be here for you."

Chapter 24

Handling That Which Has Been Handed to You

■ ■ ■ ■

Have you ever prayed to God, asking for the opportunity to get to know Him more? Have you read Scripture and affirmed the statement that He must increase and you must decrease? Have you ever asked God to take you to a deeper place, hoping to become more like Him and experience a part of life you never have? Have you ever commented to yourself that you want to learn more about Him and about life? Have you ever told God that you want to be more like Him? Have you asked Him to expand your territory?

Now let me ask you this. If you asked God for any of those things, did you think He would grant your request without providing some further training? And did you think that training was going to be easy? When He began to answer your questions, did you ever think that the opportunity to grow in these ways would include parenting a teenage son or daughter?

Probably not.

I think God teaches us more about Himself through suffering than He does through fun and exciting experiences. And we probably listen better when we're in pain. Of course, we listen because we want some relief from our pain. God surely uses all of it, allows more than we could ever imagine, and is there to comfort us through all the pain we experience.

I can now see God's faithfulness to me in the past. I look back at situations in my life that were so difficult at the time, and I now see His hand, His purpose, and His intent. Looking back at my life without any rose-colored glasses, I see that it has been tough and that He has been good. Because of what I have seen, I am able to project into the future that the days ahead will be like this as well. I stand on His promises, I'm assured of His presence, I love His involvement, and I know beyond a shadow of a doubt that He will cause all things to work together for good.

But I don't live in the past or in the future. I live today, and today is difficult.

In the present, on this day, many parents feel as if they are losing what they value most—their son or daughter. Their child is struggling, and that makes the struggle of this day doubly hard. A child who struggles affects the whole family and leaves no member untouched.

Feelings of pain may lead to feelings that God has abandoned you in the midst of your struggle. Feeling isolated and alone, you may think you've done something wrong and are being excluded from His presence. Not knowing what to do for your child in the midst of the turmoil, you may feel as if you're being punished. You might feel like the victim of someone else's issues. When struggle of any sort happens within your family, a cavalcade of feelings will arise. Having these feelings is okay. They are what they are. But I want to encourage you that God has not forgotten about you, nor has He abandoned you. He's probably using all of this pain to fulfill the very things you have asked for.

When you asked God to bring someone into your life to transform you more into His image, did you think that He would use a son spinning out of control or a daughter struggling with same-sex relationship issues to do so? Let me tell you something I believe in strongly: He does, and He will.

I had a dream a few years ago that changed my perspective on a number of things. I'm not a big dreamer, and I am hardly an interpreter of dreams. But this dream needed no interpretation. It was a clear statement to me. For many, many years I have felt a little anger toward someone who never gave me what I thought he could give, never supported me when I wanted his support, and never connected with me in a relational way. My expectations were high, his performance was low, and I was disappointed most of my adult life. I was angry at times, disappointed at other times, and bitter some of the time, and I always felt a great loss from that relationship.

I dreamed that I died and went to heaven. As I approached God, I surprisingly noticed that a person who had caused some of my greatest disappointment in life was standing next to Him. I sarcastically asked God, "What is he doing here?"

God answered gently, "Mark, I have been using this person in your life to make you into the person that I want you to be." When I woke up the next morning, a great burden had been lifted from me as I realized that I had been fighting most of my life with God's tool to mold me into the person He wants me to be. Quite honestly, I wonder if I would be doing all the ministry things I'm doing now had it not been for the events and feelings, as painful as they were, that I experienced as a result of this person being in my life.

There's a bigger picture in God's camera than the snapshot you stare at most of the time. Indeed, He uses people in your life, and just as iron sharpens iron, one man, one son, or one daughter might just sharpen you.

God will also use you in other people's lives. As you learn and grow through conflict and pain, other people learn in similar ways. Perhaps the conflict you are working through has been orchestrated by God to bring change in another person's life. God may be using you to be the one to stand in the gap and move people where He wants them to be. Maybe God intends for a person to be in your life because He knows you can go the distance with her and fight the good fight that she needs to make her into the woman she'll need to be when she gets married, has kids, and becomes an adult. You didn't think that the helmet of salvation, the breastplate of righteousness, the belt of truth, the shield of faith, and the shoes of the gospel were intended just to make you look good, did you?

The battle gear we wear is not for some Christian fashion show; it is for doing battle for the souls of sons and daughters. It's what you have prepared for. It is what He has prepared you for. To deny or avoid your involvement would only thwart the plan that God has in store for you both.

A young man I know who has wrestled with depression, anger, alcoholism, and selfish rage recently told me of a major change in his life. He realized that everything in his life wasn't anyone else's fault. For years, he had fought his mom and dad, thinking they had caused him to be a mess. His comment was simple. He said, "You gotta play the cards you're dealt." For some, those could have been words of resignation. Perhaps they were. But for me, they were words of accepting responsibility for his life, and they empowered him to work through his issues rather than avoiding them or postponing them for later.

He accepted what was before him and the responsibility that accompanied that enlightenment—at the end of a ten-year fight with his dad. I am grateful that this dad never gave up and continued to fight the good fight for his son. It wasn't easy, and most of it wasn't fun, but it was worthwhile. This dad told me that he always knew that to help someone change, we must first love that person. He said that he always loved his son, even though there were days that he wanted to kill him. He shared how distraught he had gotten at times and how he took his anger out on his wife and his coworkers. His acknowledgment that God was using his son to change some things in his life was amazing to me. We've cried and laughed together through the years of struggling through his hardships with his son, and both are better for it. Perhaps a little more like the people they wanted to become and a little more like the Man who put them together in the first place.

I told the dad that his role should be to stand strong with his son and to keep looking for ways he needed to change. The log in his eye became more important than the speck in his son's eye. He asked God to search his heart and point out any areas in his life where he had been hurtful to his son or his family, and he chose to take care of his own stuff when it was revealed to him.

When a parent admits his own fault and wrongdoing, the ways he has hurt people, and his formerly unrepentant heart, he gives his child an example and the freedom to do what is needed to restore relationships. Over time, if done with a spirit of humility, the admission of wrongdoing is inviting and eliminates the possibility of performance-based relationship, which is what most teens expect when they want to live up to their parents' expectations. Set an example, empower your teen, and set the stage for a different and deeper relationship.

Here's a Scripture to remember as you embrace the bigger picture for your life and the life of your family. It is one for all parents to hold on to. God invites you to take the hand of your teen and lead him to a deeper relationship with Him and with you: "I am still confident of this: I will see the goodness of the LORD in the land of the living" (Psalm 27:13).

Chapter 25

What's Happening to My Teen?

■ ■ ■ ■

I t's a question I've been asked hundreds of times. Parents want to know what is happening to their teen, and many parents of younger preteens are worried about what will happen as their child enters those turbulent teen years. Many parents are afraid because they have watched friends raise their kids with the best intentions, get involved in their kids' lives, and do all the right things, only to see their teen struggle when she hit the adolescent years. Parents can feel as if regardless of how well they do, their child might still struggle during her teen years. And that is true. There are no guarantees. There is no special equation of parenting skills that equals success.

But families who go through difficult times aren't always in a bad place just because a child struggles with the challenges of adolescence. Struggles create opportunities for parents to teach their children about a faith that will sustain them even in the midst of conflict. How parents fare in the struggle is a far better measure of good parenting than whether a family struggles at all.

The hardship you fear might provide the chance to grow deeper and closer to your teen. The conflict you want to avoid might open the door to maturity and responsibility. The uncertainty you face might be the new window of opportunity you have been seeking.

Your teen needs you desperately. He is influenced by a culture that is difficult at best. If you're not there to counter its effect, who will be?

He is exposed to things that call for you to establish new values and solidify others. Who will help him form these new perspectives? Your teen will make choices that will affect the rest of his life, and he will be affected by the choices that others will make. Will you be there to help him sort through the wheat and the chaff? If the upcoming teen years scare the daylights out of you, what do you think they are doing to your teen? Teens need you—in conflict, in struggle, and especially when it is very hard.

Chances are that the issues you are concerned about for your child are not confined to one chapter in this book. I'm sure most people face a combination of issues and a variety of challenges. I doubt that any child exactly matches the people I have told stories about in this book. I hope that you will pull principles from each of the stories and look at all the strategies before applying a list to your own situation. You need a well-developed strategy to help your child during his teen years. The issues you could face are never simple, so don't think just one thing in this book will revolutionize anyone's life.

There are no easy answers, but there are some pretty successful strategies that have worked in the lives of many families who have carefully and intentionally pursued them. An old Yiddish proverb says, "What you don't see with your eyes, don't invent with your mouth." I have followed that advice in this book. What I have seen is what you have read. My shotgun approach of telling many stories was intended to give you the opportunity to put together little tidbits of each and write your own chapter that will apply to your own teen, your own situation, and your own needs. My hope is that you will connect with a combination of issues and couple that with a combination of solutions in order to put together a unique plan for your teen and your family.

Allow me to reiterate a few themes that are vital to your family's success:

First, your involvement is the key to your child's success. My goal for kids is to get to the other side of adolescence with relationships intact. Of course, you want to keep collateral damage to a minimum. But the relationship you have with your teen is of utmost importance.

Second, I hope that you will convey a true and accurate description of who God is to your child and that you will accentuate your teaching in her younger years with actions that validate all that you have taught. A young lady named Bri once told me, "If you believe in God, it's just one more person to disappoint." She was the angriest girl I have ever met. A teen's perspective of God is formed in her early years. Her commitment to Him is developed in her teen years. And usually, her concept of a relationship with Christ is "caught" from what she sees in her parents.

Finally, would you be to your teen who God is to you? I heard James Taylor say this on a CBS Sunday morning interview: "You can change people...unconditional love on a daily basis can melt a stone." There's no reason for me to add anything else to his wisdom.

The first year I became a parent, I decided to go see what all these 40-year-old women I was working with were screaming about. He was called the King of Rock n' Roll. Elvis Presley. I just wanted to see what all the buzz was about and watch the production of his show. I recognized most of his songs, watched people throw flowers up on the stage, and heard the clamor when he threw them a sweaty towel (that was weird). He did a whole lot of shakin', talked about a party in the county jail, and told us all what wise men say. It was a good show. What amazed me most was when the "King" ended his show and walked off stage. A voice announced on the PA system, "Elvis has left the building," proving that he was not a king. Everything stopped. It was over. He was gone. The excitement quit, and people started filing out of the building. It was done. He wasn't coming back, and all we were left with was ringing ears, sweaty towels, overpriced T-shirts, and a good memory. Elvis had left the building.

You know what I've thought during the 30 years since I saw that concert? A real king would never leave. My King says, "Never will I leave you; never will I forsake you" (Hebrews 13:5).

God has not left what He is building!

More Great Harvest House Books for Parents

When Your Teen Is Struggling
Mark Gregston

If your teen is exhibiting destructive or unhealthy behaviors and actions, Mark Gregston offers you biblical guidance, encouraging stories, and a fresh message of hope as he shares the keys to turn struggle to success.

Authentic Parenting in a Postmodern Culture
Mary DeMuth

With sensitivity and grace, Mary DeMuth describes the new way people are processing truth. She reveals effective ways you can communicate with today's kids: by developing relationships, by learning along with your kids, by creating a safe haven for them to explore their worlds, and more.

MySpace®, MyKids
Jason Illian

Boasting more that 75 million users when this book was written, the MySpace online community was the second most visited site on the Internet. Should you be concerned? Jason Illian demonstrates that with careful use and close monitoring, MySpace can help kids facilitate relationships and help parents interact with their children's world like never before.

When Good Kids Make Bad Choices
Elyse Fitzpatrick, James Newheiser, and Laura Hendrickson

Three qualified biblical counselors share how you can deal with the emotional trauma of a child going astray. This heartfelt and practical guide includes excellent advice regarding medicines commonly prescribed to children.

When Your Child Is Hurting
Glynnis Whitwer

Glynnis Whitwer identifies many of the painful experiences children face—harsh reprimands, uncaring remarks, troubling misunderstandings—and gives parents practical, effective advice to handle these painful situations. Warm and encouraging, filled with heartfelt inspiration, each chapter includes real-life stories and study questions for groups or personal devotions.